Suddenly, several VC came storming around a bend in one of the other trails entering our position. Unfortunately, they found themselves staring straight down the muzzle of our M-60 from a distance of less than twenty meters. Expecting to hear the sweet chattering of the M-60, we were stupefied when we heard the sound of a single *click*. The machine gun would not fire! Reacting as one, we began popping them with M-16s and CAR-15s.

Things started to escalate as the enemy returned fire. Over the next few minutes, it got so intense that we had to call in artillery. When the 105mm rounds began impacting among the enemy positions, the VC moved in closer to our positions to avoid the deadly shells. They were not stupid. They knew that we could bring in the artillery only so close without endangering ourselves. So, already low on ammo and in dire straits ourselves, we did the last thing the enemy expected—we called in the artillery almost directly on top of our positions. . . .

WAR PAINT

Bill Goshen

BALLANTINE BOOKS • NEW YORK

A Ballantine Book
Published by The Ballantine Publishing Group
Copyright © 2001 by Bill Goshen
Foreword copyright © 2001 by Don Smith
Introduction copyright © 2001 by Carl Cook

Scripture quotations marked (NLT) are taken from the Holy Bible, New Living Translation, copyright © 1996. Used by permission of Tyndale House Publishers, Inc., Wheaton, Illinois 60189. All rights reserved.

www.ballantinebooks.com

ISBN 0-345-44491-4

Manufactured in the United States of America

First Edition: November 2001

10 9 8 7 6 5 4 3 2 1

Wall Talk

by Bill Goshen

Hey, Bob—Yeah, Gary!
What's going on out there;
Look at this crowd around us,
Talking, crying, and whispering prayers.

Say, Gary—Yeah, Bob!
What kind of meeting is this?
Soldiers, Marines, sailors, and guard,
And beaucoup civilians visiting us.

Touching us with their hands
With heaviness in their hearts;
We speak to them in response,
But it seems we're in the dark!

Traveling these United States
Concealed in this granite wall,
Carrying out our duties,
Answering our nation's call.

Why don't these people hear us
As we seek to join with them,
Locked in this granite prison,
Separated from family and friends?

Hey, Bob—Yeah, Gary!
Some in this crowd I know.
He walked point on my team,
Seems like an eternity ago.

See that lady over there
With tears flowing down her face.
She was a nurse in triage
In MASH at Lai Khe base.

Hey, Gary—Yeah, Bob!
You reckon this is just a dream,
Reflecting off our minds,
Producing this emotional scene.

Say, Bob—Yeah, Gary!
What if it's really true?
Could we have died in combat,
Serving the Red, White, and Blue?

You must be right about that,
Most of them are grieving.
No wonder they can't hear us,
Look at the items they're leaving.

Old letters, mementos from the past
That remind them when we were alive.
Vets with so many physical wounds,
Agonizing deeply inside.

Rumor says we lost the war,
Though we won every major battle.
The politicians stopped us from going to Hanoi
And forcing the Commies to settle.

Why did they keep us from triumph,
And seemingly accept defeat,
Leaving all the South Vietnamese
To be slaughtered in their retreat?

Hey, Bob—What's that, Gary?
At least America remembers us all
Who went in the name of freedom
When Uncle Sam gave the call.

Maybe our country learned something from Nam,
And history will not repeat,
If we must fight, fight to win,
And let politicians be discreet.

Notice the youth who are passing by,
Asking why so many died.
Maybe they will live in liberty,
And their mamas won't have to cry.

America, if anyone can hear us,
We are freedom's cost.
Love and protect it with all that you have,
Lest you find your freedom is lost!

Contents

Acknowledgments   xi
Foreword   xiii
Introduction   xvii
Author's Note   xxi
Map   xxiv
Chapter 1: All the Way   1
Chapter 2: Imagine That!   17
Chapter 3: The Buscapade   20
Chapter 4: Ant Bush   25
Chapter 5: The Phantom Factor   28
Chapter 6: Peace and War   31
Chapter 7: Twin Cobras   33
Chapter 8: Red Alert   36
Chapter 9: Unwelcome Committee   41
Chapter 10: War Paint   44
Chapter 11: Peekaboo   48
Chapter 12: Covey of Quail   52
Chapter 13: The Night Stalkers   55
Chapter 14: Seeing Is Believing   67
Chapter 15: Remember the Alamo   71
Chapter 16: The Twilight Zone   78
Chapter 17: Mission Impossible   81
Chapter 18: Snake Bit   84
Chapter 19: Wake-up Call   87
Chapter 20: The Tragic Truth   92

Contents

Chapter 21: Roaming the Woods   98
Chapter 22: Too Much Pain   101
Chapter 23: Tropical Menagerie   104
Chapter 24: Bombs Away   107
Chapter 25: Bits 'n' Pieces   112
Chapter 26: A Caged Tiger   116
Chapter 27: A Recondo Christmas   122
Chapter 28: Nightmare Eve, 1968   129
Chapter 29: Melancholy Moments   133
Chapter 30: The Hot Spot   136
Chapter 31: Ambush Bay   139
Chapter 32: Zoology 101 R.V.N.   141
Chapter 33: Changing Colors   144
Chapter 34: The Rising Sun   147
Chapter 35: A Giant Good-bye   150
Chapter 36: Law's Legacy   153
Chapter 37: The Longest Night   157
Chapter 38: BAMC 43-C   170
Chapter 39: Purple Haze   179
Chapter 40: The Quan Loi Fiasco   183
Chapter 41: The Long Road Back   187
Chapter 42: Smorgasbord   192
Chapter 43: Feelings   196
            The Last Team   199
            Echoes of Freedom   201
            Postscript   205
            Appendix A   207
            Appendix B   209
            Appendix C   211
            Glossary   215
            Index   227

Acknowledgments

This book will certainly be lacking if I don't honor and thank some very special individuals.

First, to all you redlegs who fired support for us so many times; your speed and accuracy was always appreciated. You kept us from being wiped out on many an occasion. Few realized the danger you faced manning those small firebases out in the boonies. You were always open to attack yourselves and certainly in harm's way. Thank you. We remember you and honor your tremendous courage, expertise, and dedication.

Second, to the crews of the helicopters who supported us, you were simply awesome. Gunships, slicks, scouts, medevacs, and pararescue, you all did a wonderful job getting us out of trouble. You saved our bacon many times. We had a special relationship with you, and still do. We salute and honor you courageous men.

Third, to all the fighter, bomber, FAC, and air-relay crews who showed such great skill and fortitude. We owe you our lives. Thank you for going the extra mile.

Fourth, to the aerorifle platoons and you grunt line doggies who came charging in to rescue us when we bit off more than we could chew, we give you our most sincere thanks. Many times you paid a heavy price coming to our aid. We will never forget you.

Fifth, to all you "Lurp"-Rangers that served with me, I

will never forget you. You will always be in my fondest memories. This certainly includes Larry Wenzel, the only other survivor of our team.

Then, to my parents, brothers, and sister who prayed for and encouraged me with those cards, letters, and goodies, I thank you from the bottom of my heart.

Next, to my loving wife and children who have weathered the storm with me, I love you forever! Jackie, without your time, effort, and many hours, days, and months working on the computer, *War Paint* would not be a reality. Just as you are my helper in all our daily affairs, you are a major source and inspiration in this project.

Additionally, to my friend, agent, and coeditor, Gary Linderer, I heartily thank you for all the guidance and hard work you have put into this enormous endeavor. Without your expertise as a former Lurp-Ranger and author, this book would be lacking and probably unfinished. Also, thanks to Owen Lock for believing in this book, and to Christopher Evans for being so helpful.

Finally, to the Lord Jesus Christ who is responsible for my survival, sanity, and salvation, I express my deepest love and loyalty throughout eternity.

Foreword

by Sgt. Don Smith, USA (Ret.)

Vietnam, 0200 hours, the dry season at an artillery firebase somewhere in III Corps:

It is quiet and dark. The silence is broken by a whisper over the radio.

"Trail Spike Two-Nine, this is Panther One-Zero-Zero-Four. Over."

I reply, "Panther One-Zero-Zero-Four, this is Trail Spike Two-Nine. Go ahead."

"We have movement. Fire Delta Tango November, drop five zero zero, Hotel Echo. Over."

The reply is two clicks on the handset, meaning affirmative. We compute the data and give it to the gun crews manning the six 105mm howitzers. The captain notifies the FDC (fire direction center) that the guns are ready.

The FDC says, "Splash. Over."

Panther One-Zero-Zero-Four acknowledges, "Splash. Out."

Then, silence . . . it lasts only seconds, but it seems like minutes. We hear the impact echo through the night, then I hear a low whisper over the radio, one so low that I turn up the volume all the way and ask for a repeat.

Again, the whisper, "Drop five zero zero and give us a three by three Hotel Echo, over." I repeat the correction. Panther whispers, "Fire on my command. Over."

I acknowledge with a simple "Ten four. Good luck." I say

good luck because the rounds will land right on top of them. At least, they know they are coming. The fire mission is given and the battery waits for the command to fire. I must give that command. The captain wants to know why we are waiting, so I ask Panther.

He whispers, "Gooks too close." There is a short pause, then he says, "Fire on one click."

I acknowledge with two clicks of my own. The wait continues. Finally, I get a single click over the radio. I quickly "Roger" with two clicks, then turn and give the command, "Battery fire."

"Splash. Over."

They answer my message with two clicks. We listen as each howitzer fires nine times, sending fifty-four rounds with a fifty-meter dispersion of three down and three across that saturates an area 150 by 200 meters square. Then silence prevails as we wait.

After some time, I call, "Panther One-Zero-Zero-Four, this is Trail Spike Two-Nine. Over."

There is no response.

Again I call them, but no answer comes. Only silence over the handset. The firebase grows quiet again except for the normal sounds of the jungle. FDC personnel are released to go back to bed. We are underground, covered by PSP sheets and layers of sandbags with only one small opening to go in and out.

I turn off the battery-operated spotlight that illuminates the charts and radio equipment. Now I am in total darkness. As I rest on my cot, my mind races with questions. On our chart, they were just a number, a voice on the radio asking for help. Usually, it was a LRP team, or a Special Forces team, or maybe a SEAL or SOG team. We never knew and seldom found out the results of our fire missions.

In Bill Goshen's *War Paint*, you will get a glimpse into the lives of the special operators who worked in small teams that always went in harm's way. Bill is one of those men, whom I have known for more than twenty years. He received a Purple Heart and a Silver Star for valor. The award should have been higher.

This book unlocks the secrecy and raw courage of America's valiant, unconventional warriors. Courage is not the action of one who is unafraid; it entails overcoming fear in order to accomplish a task. Bill's story exemplifies that truth. His book comes from his heart, revealing a man who was willing to die for his team. He kept going all the way when others might have laid down and died. He has paid a high price for his tour of duty in Vietnam.

Bill was "written off," at first. Then, when he survived, they said he would never walk again. He proved them wrong on both accounts. Today, Bill does walk, but his gait is a constant reminder of Vietnam. Each day, he deals with the pain of wounds in his hip, back, arms, shoulder, and mind. He met death face-to-face, and with the help of God's grace, he has won.

This book is a true account of the life of a Vietnam-era LRP/Ranger who fought for his country when his country called. It is a testimonial worth reading and rereading, a keeper for sure. Read it and learn about the heavy cost of living in "the land of the free and the home of the brave." I was there with the 1st Cavalry Division, firing those 105s as a "redleg" artillery trooper.

Introduction

by Sgt. Maj. Carl Cook, USA (Ret.)

This book certainly needed to be written. It details the exploits of a LRP/Ranger and his unit serving in the Vietnam combat theater, allowing the reader to understand how the LRP/Ranger organizations operated in that war. The reader can see—even feel—what it was like through the author's own true-life experiences in combat. This is the real thing, a true story of the hardships, the bonding, the commitment, and the love these warriors had for one another.

I was assigned as the unit first sergeant from late October 1968 until April 1969. Bill Goshen was an excellent soldier. He was professional, intelligent, and displayed strong leadership qualities. He spent a lot of time keeping himself in good physical condition. And Bill always took time to pass on to the newer members of his team things he had learned as a point man.

In the chapter entitled "The Longest Night," Bill sensed that the patrol he was assigned to would be a difficult mission due to the last-minute formation of the team, the mission it was confronted with, and the fact that the men had never worked together as a team before. Knowing full well that it would probably be a very tough experience, Bill still accepted the assignment. After that incredibly difficult, heartrending mission was over, I personally wrote up a recommendation for him to receive the Distinguished Service

Cross. Years later, I found out that he had been awarded the Silver Star instead.

Company F, 52d Infantry (LRP) was redesignated Company I, 75th Infantry (Ranger) on February 1, 1969. I must say that it was the finest unit that I served with during my twenty years of active service in the United States Army. I turned down another assignment in order to become a member of that outstanding unit; I wanted to serve with a top-notch outfit that operated in small teams.

Although we went through some rocky times, and a few people who did not fit, we were a solid, professional group of volunteers. We carried out many dangerous—sometimes disastrous—assignments as the "eyes and ears" of the Big Red One—the 1st Infantry Division. Our long-range patrols were burdened by hardship, deprivation, and personal sacrifice. But someone had to be the scouts for the larger units. Our men exemplified the 1st Infantry Division motto, "No mission too difficult, no sacrifice too great, duty first."

I cannot begin to express in words what my heart feels for the gallant young Americans who served as members of the long-range reconnaissance patrols, the long-range patrols, and the Rangers. All gave some; some gave all. And most performed incredible feats without receiving the recognition they deserved.

Vietnam was a much different type of war from those that preceded it. My first combat came during the Korean War, at the age of eighteen. That experience helped me to understand what the young men serving in Vietnam were going through even though the style of warfare was so vastly different from that we faced in Korea. The Korean War saw fighting along an established MLR, or main line of resistance. We knew that, for the most part, everything to our front was enemy-controlled. Everything behind us was friendly. Vietnam had no safe areas, including the large division-size base camps. In Korea, we fought major actions across a broad front. When the Chinese Army entered the war, they attacked across the open in hordes.

Vietnam, however, was a war of small-unit operations and

guerrilla tactics, and our LRPs worked in small teams, usually consisting of six men. They were very disciplined and possessed a strong camaraderie. The movies gave Vietnam veterans a bad rap. They were not a mob of drug-addicted, crazed baby killers as Hollywood portrayed them. Occasionally someone of that kind did pop up, just as happened in all wars, but the men who served in Vietnam were every bit as good as those who served in World War II and Korea.

The politicians interfered in the war in Vietnam just as they did in Korea. And it was common for staff officers not to believe the accurate intelligence gathered by our patrols, which resulted in our members being killed and wounded. Occasionally, it cost us entire teams. Sending small units to accomplish what large infantry companies should be doing is always costly. We were constantly on the hot seat, and our men met the challenge head-on.

I served proudly in Korea and Vietnam, but my LRPs and Rangers led the way.

Author's Note

Remembering incidents that occurred about thirty years ago is at times very easy and, likewise, at times hard. I have attempted to write as accurately as possible, from my perspective, the way events took place during my tour of duty.

This is the story of some unique men of all colors and walks of life. Bonded by triumph and tragedy, by life and death, we became very close to our team members.

This book is not an argument on whether the war in Vietnam was right or wrong. *War Paint* is about young men, mostly nineteen- to twenty-two-year-olds, who were sent to become warriors without a cause. It soon became obvious we were not going to be allowed to show our might and defeat the enemy as our dads and uncles had in World War II!

Politics and politicians are often difficult to understand. When your government sends you to battle, you go. "Theirs not to reason why, theirs but to do and die," Tennyson wrote.

All I know is that when you are in an environment of war, you see things from a different perspective than if you are merely watching it on the news. This is the first book to be written on Company F, 52d Infantry LRPs, and Company I, 75th Infantry Rangers; we served the 1st Infantry Division proudly in Vietnam, and our stories need to be told.

It is my hope that you will see America's best giving their

all while being ridiculed back home. The anguish of it all never leaves us; we all gave some, but *some gave all*!

To POWs, MIAs, and their families

The agony and torment of feeling abandoned by one's country can be understood only by those who experience it! As well, hunger, thirst, torture, and inhumane treatment in deplorable living conditions can be fully fathomed only by those who endure the same.

The great price you are paying for freedom can never be compensated for. To those families that endure despite the loss of loved ones, you have experienced pain beyond what others can understand. All we can say is thank you all for the sacrifices you make for the United States of America.

We will not forget! God bless you, and let freedom ring!

To America's youth

This book presents a challenge to the youth, our future leaders, to carry the torch of freedom throughout this new century.

What part will you play in life to be a productive citizen, contributing to your fellow Americans and to freedom?

Many have different ideas about war, especially about the one fought in Vietnam! My intentions are not to justify, condone, or condemn our part in that war, but to show a perspective many have not seen.

The men and women who served in Vietnam carry scars, physical and emotional, that you may one day have to bear!

I hate war and its atrocities, but I love freedom more passionately. Is living under bondage really living?

Our government sent us, and we went. Does that make us villains or victims? Try to put yourselves in our shoes after reading, and understand some of what we have gone through.

Finally, it is my desire that, if you must experience combat, you go for the right reason, that is, to protect freedom and families. And may you go to win, with the government and citizens' full support. If we must fight, winning must be the objective!

To the veterans

What can we say to you for your service and sacrifice on behalf of the United States of America? Thank you! Whether you served in combat or not, you served.

Leaving your family and friends and spending many lonely months away is a sacrifice of service. I, for one, appreciate you!

To all who served in combat in all wars and so-called conflicts—your sacrifices are many and painful. Thank you so very much for freedom!

To my fellow Vietnam combat vets—I stand with you in memory of the horrible ordeals and in the feeling of abandonment by those who sent us but would not allow us to win.

We served faithfully and never lost a major battle, but our hands were cuffed by politicians who controlled us like pawns in a chess match. War is not a game.

All of us gave some, indeed, but may we never forget that *some gave all*!

This book is dedicated to you and to them. Thank you for going, giving, and getting the satisfaction of knowing how precious freedom, family, and friends really are!

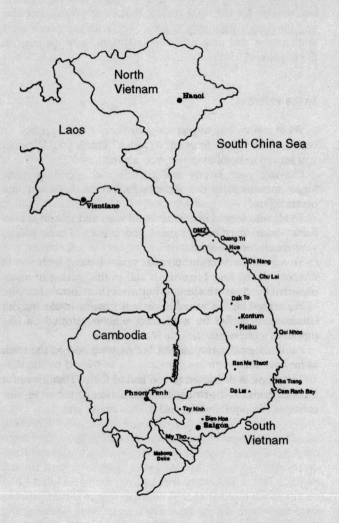

North
Vietnam

Laos

Hanoi

South China Sea

Vientiane

DMZ
Quang Tri
Hue
Da Nang
Chu Lai

Dak To
Kontum
Pleiku
Qui Nhon

Cambodia

Ban Me Thuot

Phnom Penh

Nha Trang
Cam Ranh Bay

Da Lat

Tay Ninh
Bien Hoa
Saigon

South
Vietnam

My Tho

Mekong
Delta

Chapter 1

All the Way

On August 28, 1948, something happened to me that would affect my entire existence on this planet called Earth—I was born! Tulsa, Oklahoma, added me to its census that evening; my parents picked up another tax exemption.

Since I've been old enough to remember, adventure and excitement have always captured my attention. Westerns and war movies were my favorites, and I loved it when the Earps beat the Clantons to the draw at the OK Corral, and the Marines mowed down the Japanese human-wave assaults on Guadalcanal. It was the way of the warrior—the way it was supposed to be done.

I still remember Hopalong Cassidy mounted on the back of his snow-white stallion, Topper, as he passed by me during a parade down the streets of Tulsa, Oklahoma. Because I got to see him in person, he was always one of my favorites.

There were also Roy Rogers, Gene Autry, Davy Crockett, and Daniel Boone. They were all special to me—they were my heroes. John Wayne, Gary Cooper, Alan Ladd, and Randolph Scott were my favorite tough guys. Crockett, Boone, and Jim Bowie fascinated me, causing me to feel that I had been shortchanged at birth. I convinced myself that I should have been born during the early frontier days. Wearing my coonskin cap and carrying a rifle like Crockett's old Betsy, I would have wreaked havoc on the frontier.

1

For hours at a time, my childhood friends and I played cowboys and Indians; then we would switch to being combat soldiers during World War II, using sticks as weapons if guns were not available. Many battles raged daily through our neighborhood, and the good guys always won. It was about then that the series *Combat* was running on television, and it commanded most of my attention. I especially liked the theme song.

At an early age, my first BB gun was a constant companion, and then, on my sixth birthday, I was given the ultimate weapon—a single-shot .22-caliber rifle. After drilling me with an extended course in gun safety and showing me how to care for it, my dad taught me how to shoot. We spent many hours rabbit and squirrel hunting along the Arkansas River. Those times hold some of my fondest early memories.

My parents divorced when I was almost seven, and both remarried shortly afterward. I stayed with my mom and my stepdad, and when I turned eight, they moved us to Irving, Texas. We stayed there for six years before relocating again to Hurst, Texas, where I attended L.D. Bell High School.

Summer-league baseball and football occupied much of my time during my high school years. In addition, I swam, played a lot of golf, and fished. All those activities were fun, but my real love was hunting. I could hardly wait until the seasons opened in the fall. Quail, dove, rabbit, squirrel, and deer were my favorites.

After I graduated from high school, my career path seemed unclear. I considered coaching or being a government hunter or game warden, but nothing really seemed very appealing. I wanted to work outdoors, but everything I looked at seemed to lack the adventure and excitement I craved. I enrolled at North Texas State University at Denton in the fall. However, I suffered a thigh injury while playing touch football that put me on crutches for a while. The temporary disability didn't do much for my motivation, and after struggling to make it through the semester, I decided to return home and enlist in the army.

Right after I got back home, Steve Gerber, a friend from

high school, came home from Vietnam on a thirty-day extension leave. He was in Special Forces (SF), and he was going back for six more months. After spending some quality time talking with him and reading a brochure about SF, I decided that it was just the challenge I had been looking for. Steve gave me a ride on the back of his motorcycle, and the two of us headed to Arlington, Texas, to talk to an army recruiter. It didn't take him long to convince me that the army was where I belonged. I enlisted for Special Forces and departed for basic combat training at Fort Polk, Louisiana, in October 1967.

I was in excellent physical condition when I reported for basic. That, and the fact that I had a very positive attitude, enabled me to come within one point of being the outstanding trainee of my basic-training cycle. Still, it got me a promotion to private E-2. After graduation, I was transferred to Fort Huachuca, Arizona, to attend Morse code school, a critical MOS (military occupational specialty), for Special Forces.

Two weeks before graduation, my dad was killed in an automobile accident. I went home on emergency leave to attend the funeral. By the time I returned to Fort Huachuca, my class had already graduated. Fortunately, one only had to send and receive thirteen words a minute to graduate from the course. Since I was already sending and receiving twenty-three words per minute, they gave me my certificate immediately.

Fort Benning, Georgia, was my next stop. I had already made the decision to attend Airborne school as soon as I finished Morse code classes. The very thought of being a paratrooper excited me, though I had always been afraid of heights. I arrived a few days before our class actually started, so I had the distinct pleasure of serving on KP, an experience not worth telling about. It was not an enjoyable episode.

Airborne training officially began on a Monday with ground week, mental harassment, and physical conditioning, which meant run, run, run, everywhere we went. Obviously, it was an attempt by the cadre to run the less committed trainees into quitting. A few did. We also practiced our PLFs (parachute landing falls) to make sure that if the fall didn't kill us, we could survive the landing. We also practiced exiting the aircraft properly. This was important because a bad exit could result in a number of major problems when a chute opens, any of which could result in a crash-and-burn arrival on the drop zone 1,250 feet below. The commands of "stand up," "hook up," and "shuffle to the door" were drummed into our heads over and over again.

Week two, tower week, consisted of training on the 34-foot and 250-foot towers. The first simulated the shock of the parachute opening, and the second gave us a taste of falling under a full canopy. They separated the men from the boys and gave us a sample of what we would be experiencing during an actual jump.

Finally, jump week was upon us, the climax to the previous two weeks' training. That was the week that would see us making five actual parachute jumps, the number needed to qualify for the coveted jump wings of a paratrooper. Quite a few guys washed out of the program during that critical week in our training, and our jump class was significantly smaller as we approached graduation day. What a rush it was to stand in the door and fling myself up and out into the prop blast! When the chute opened seconds later and I looked up to see that oversize canopy fully deployed, there was no thrill like it anywhere on the face of the earth.

When we graduated after our fifth jump, Colonel Welch, the Airborne School commandant, congratulated us and welcomed us into the elite airborne brotherhood. I was pleasantly surprised to discover that I had been promoted to the rank of private first class (E-3) right after graduation.

I took the Special Forces battery test, a four-hour written exam, shortly after completing Jump School. I was informed the next day that my scores were acceptable and that I was off to Special Forces Training Group at Fort Bragg, North Carolina.

Fort Bragg was only a short distance out of Fayetteville, North Carolina, and was also the home of the 82d Airborne

Division and the XVIII Airborne Corps. When we arrived, we were bused out to Smoke Bomb Hill and assigned to Training Group. I was excited that I would soon be able to wear the green beret and crest emblazoned with the motto *De Oppresso Liber*—We Liberate the Oppressed, but we had to complete three separate and very demanding phases of training before graduating and getting our group beret flash.

Phase I was a mixture of physical conditioning, classroom training, and a survival exercise that involved a parachute deployment into a guerrilla-held area. The classroom training was interesting and germane to what we would be doing in the field. After completing the round of instruction, we were ready for the coming exercise.

The survival exercise was to be a lesson in military tactics, conditioning, and endurance. We would begin the exercise by making a night parachute jump into a small drop zone. While being pursued by aggressor forces for several days, we would be forced to live off the land while navigating through thick, heavily forested terrain. We would have to practice patrol techniques, do immediate-action drills, and establish ambushes as we had been taught in the classroom phase of our training.

During the jump, my stick was the last one to exit the aircraft into the pitch-black night. Everything went well until I was about treetop high, when I was caught by a strong crosswind that turned my chute and hurtled me into the ground. I landed hard, flat on my back in the middle of an asphalt road with a full load of equipment on. The impact nearly knocked me unconscious. When I was finally able to gather my wits about me, I discovered that I suffered a numbing paralysis. My back was throbbing, and the pain was unbearable.

An ambulance arrived to evacuate me to Womack Army Hospital, where doctors diagnosed my injury as a lower lumbar back strain. They ordered several days of bed rest, followed by a period of physical therapy. My world was shattered soon afterward when I was informed that my dream of being SF-qualified was very much in doubt. If I could ever jump again, I would surely have to be recycled back through Phase I to start over again. However, my back continued to bother me even though I had decided to drive on.

Word soon filtered down to Training Group that 5th Special Forces Group needed more personnel in Vietnam. Several of us volunteered to terminate Training Group and go directly to Vietnam in hopes of getting into 5th Group. After a thirty-day leave, I flew out of Dallas's Love Field for Oakland, California, on the first leg of the journey to Vietnam.

Flying on a commercial airplane for over twenty hours gave me plenty of time to reflect on my past and consider my future. Having just turned twenty years old a little over a month before, I had nearly two decades to look back over.

Family, school, sports, friends, mistakes, and achievements flooded through my mind as I stared out the aircraft window. Below us was the bright blue expanse of the Pacific Ocean. I saw an occasional ship plying the surface en route to some distant port. Inside the plane, everyone seemed lost in thoughts of home and what lay before us. It was hard to focus on anything but that strange, distant land called "Vietnam." What would the future hold for me? Would I survive the next year? After a period of time, I got tired of trying to answer the unanswerable and drifted off to sleep.

We landed at Tan Son Nhut Airport near Saigon. When I stepped off the aircraft, I was greeted by a terrific blast of heat that made me gasp. The strange smell of diesel fumes and a mixture of other noxious gases nearly overwhelmed me.

We boarded a string of olive-drab military buses for the short but scenic ride out to Bien Hoa, and then on to Long Binh, where we were turned over to the confusion and frustration of the 90th Replacement Center. We were awed by the sights and sounds of urban and rural South Vietnam. Poverty, perversity, pain, and suffering were evident wherever we looked. A country at war is a terrible thing to witness. But it was something we would get used to as we became a part of its scenery and participants in its fratricide. Guard towers, sandbagged bunkers, roadblocks, concertina wire, military vehicles and personnel were everywhere. If there was any doubt before that we were in a war zone, it was quickly erased by the martial aura surrounding South Vietnam's capital city. I developed a sudden lump in my throat that was not there when we landed a short time before. It was all quite sobering to a twenty-year-old soldier whose combat experience had been limited to books, movies, and childhood play. Vietnam was the real thing. I wondered what kind of mess I had gotten myself into. I knew that I would likely find out in the very near future.

The first night in country, we received a special welcome from the locals outside the perimeter. Mortar rounds began falling inside the compound. Monstrous explosions filled the night as shouts of "Incoming!" echoed through the night. Everyone ran for the nearest bunkers, where we cringed fearfully in the humid darkness, hoping that we would live to see the next day. Welcome to Vietnam!

The next day, we received orders assigning us to our units. The sergeant who called my name announced that I was being assigned to Company F, 52d Infantry (LRP), 1st Infantry Division. I listened proudly to the muffled comments of those around me, and the long, negative sighs of pity. I had already discovered that Special Forces was no longer in need of additional personnel, so I had volunteered for duty with the long-range patrol company, or LRPs. It was what I had trained for . . . hoped for . . . it was what I wanted. It was small-team warfare at its finest. Recon, ambushes, pilot rescues, POW snatches—all the things I had dreamed of were finally coming true.

Each infantry division and independent brigade in Vietnam had a LRP unit attached to it to serve as the eyes and ears of the parent unit. There were even two additional LRP companies, one each attached to I Field Force and II Field Force. The LRP units were made up of volunteers, for the most part Airborne-qualified, who had already earned a reputation in country for daring, resourcefulness, and problems with conventional military authority.

My orders assigned me to report to a base camp out in III

Corps at Lai Khe. It was the home of the Big Red One, the legendary 1st Infantry Division. I boarded a C-130 Hercules transport and flew out to Lai Khe the next day. When we landed, I discovered that Lai Khe lay in the middle of a huge rubber plantation, surrounded by an endless expanse of single-, double-, and triple-canopy jungle. Lai Khe had been nicknamed "Rocket City" for a very good reason; the enemy used it as the terminal point for hundreds of rocket and mortar attacks intended to demoralize and destroy American forces in the area.

A jeep was waiting to take me out to my unit. The LRP compound was right next to the rear area of one of the division's infantry companies. It was reassuring that we would be neighbors to another combat unit. Of course, I did not know that we would seldom see them in camp; the poor grunts spent most of their time out in the bush.

The jeep let us off in front of the first sergeant's hootch. I got out, dropped my bag, and knocked on the door. A deep, booming voice said, "Enter." When I stepped inside, it took a few seconds for my eyes to get used to the shadows, but when they finally adjusted, I found myself gazing on one of the biggest, meanest-looking men I had ever laid eyes on. The huge, dark-complexioned top NCO was exceptionally broad across the shoulders, an indicator of great physical strength. He sported a thick, black mustache that gave him an almost cynical, barbarian look. First Sgt. Fred Silva was well over three hundred pounds, and I would later discover that he was once a West Coast weight lifting champion.

"Hello, Lobcock! What can the first sergeant do for you?" he announced.

I was too dumbfounded to say anything, so I reached out as far as I could and handed him my orders. He read them silently, then looked up and welcomed me to the company. We conversed pleasantly for a few minutes, then he assigned me to a team. He told me that my new team leader was S. Sgt. Lonnie Ray, and had me wait there while he had his runner go find and fetch Sergeant Ray. When he arrived a short time later, I quickly discovered that Sergeant Ray was a tall, lean, black, friendly NCO from the deep south. He shook hands with me, then took me over to one of the large, olive-drab tents that served as barracks for the LRPs of Company F. I was surprised to find that the tents had wooden floors. Cots were arranged in an orderly fashion for sleeping, and each man had a footlocker and a personal area to call his own. The tent I was assigned to sat next to the bleachers belonging to the CIC orientation center. This was the division school in charge of indoctrinating newly arrived infantry troops to the rigors of Vietnam before they reported to their units.

Sergeant Ray introduced me to the rest of my team and made sure that I was squared away with a bunk, weapons, and equipment. Later that night, as I lay quietly on my bunk listening to the rest of the team discuss some of their previous missions, I began to realize the seriousness of what the unit was all about.

Special operations units were very different from conventional fighting forces. Certainly, both had their place in time of war. We worked in five- or six-man teams deep in enemy territory where there were no other friendly troops on the ground. During the missions we had to play hide-and-seek with the VC and NVA, except we knew that it was not a game. It was a military operation that could result in our destruction and death.

Our team practiced immediate-action drills for breaking contact with the enemy. Because of our small numbers, chance contacts with enemy units on the march always had the potential of a major catastrophe. Our only salvation was to hit first, maintain fire superiority, and effect our escape while the enemy was forced to keep heads down. By the time they got their act together and were able to respond, we had to be long gone.

We traveled to the range often to work on live firing of our weapons. Speed and marksmanship were just as important as our ability to move silently and remain invisible to the enemy.

We constantly practiced patrol techniques, using compass

and map, until we could find our way around the jungle fairly well. Not only was it critical that we knew exactly where we were at all times, it was also important to know where we had been and where we were going. We were never lost, merely temporarily disoriented.

Infiltration and exfiltration techniques were the keys to a good mission. They were the most dangerous times on any patrol. Getting in without being spotted, and getting out again without an enemy escort at the pickup zone, were the mark of an experienced and competent team.

We also did a lot of running and exercise. Everything else we did would be doomed to failure if we didn't practice proper physical conditioning. Our opposition was tough, and to defeat them at their own game in their own backyard, we had to be tougher. A seven-and-a-half-mile run around the base camp most every day after thirty minutes of PT was the cherry on the pie.

When we finished the run, we paired up and had horseback fights in the sandpit. One man jumped up on his partner's back as the rider. His partner was the horse. Once the riders were mounted, the object of the game was to pull the other riders from their horses, or run into them with enough force to knock them to the ground. Once a rider fell from his horse, or the horse went down, that team became disqualified. The last team standing was hailed the winner. It was nothing more than a great free-for-all, and was not only entertaining but also great exercise. I always managed to pair up with Vaughn Isaacs, a full-blooded American Indian we, naturally, called "Chief." I don't remember a time we ever lost.

All of those events promoted team unity and drew us together as comrades. Our lives depended on our teammates; we didn't want to have any doubts about their loyalties or their abilities.

All Lurp-Ranger units had many similarities and, conversely, a variety of differences as well. Our unit received mission warning orders from the 1st Infantry Division or one of its brigades. They briefed our company commander, and he selected one of our teams for the mission.

Usually, the team leader (TL) and assistant team leader (ATL) attended a briefing where operations and intelligence explained the overall picture and the mission goals. Then, the team leader issued a warning order to the team, alerting the men of an upcoming mission. He also told the team the basic equipment needed and the expected length of the mission.

Then the TL and assistant went on an overflight by helicopter to observe the target area. They picked out our landing zones (LZs) and pickup zones (PZs) along with potential routes of movement and rally points in case the team got separated.

After the overflight, the entire team got together for the mission briefing. They rehearsed immediate-action drills and individual responsibilities for the mission. Then they might take time to zero weapons and do final packing of equipment.

The night before the mission was always interesting. Each individual went through his own rituals. One person meditated alone, while others wrote letters home. Everybody sensed the upcoming danger, which usually made for a night of little sleep. Most teams inserted at first light, although some missions were launched an hour or so before sunset.

Before a mission, the team assembled and checked equipment carefully. Tape ensured that nothing rattled; the camo paint, mixed with mosquito repellent, was applied. Then, the time came to load up in a truck and drive to the chopper pad to wait for instructions to mount up. During the wait, suspense mounted. The old, familiar knot in the stomach appeared along with the dry throat. Some tried to joke to lighten up the stress, but that really did not ease the tension. Finally, the choppers fired up, and the team boarded for the trip to destiny.

The ideal equipment for each member was not available for our use. Usually, the TL and ATL had a map and compass. Many times, they were the *only* ones with such vital items. But every team member wore camo fatigues and jungle boots. There was a small assortment of headgear. Floppy hats, bandannas, or an occasional camo beret were the choices. Extra socks and foot powder were standard. Few men had CAR-15 (essentially, short-barreled M-16s) rifles to carry. Most of us carried M-16s or an occasional twelve-gauge shotgun. One man carried an M-79 grenade launcher as his primary weapon or as backup. Everyone carried a survival knife and a signal mirror. Usually, each person had from fifteen to twenty magazines loaded with eighteen rounds each. Some carried more. Everyone had an orange signal panel, and sometimes we carried pen flares. Usually, each team member toted approximately three smoke grenades, one white phosphorous grenade, and from five to seven fragmentation grenades.

All of us took freeze-dried LRRP rations. Water was an essential for survival, so we each carted five to seven quarts. The water weighed a lot, but the temperature, humidity, and the LRRP rats demanded it. In addition, we took halazone tablets to purify water taken from streams or craters.

Also, in the rucksack, rappelling gear and poncho liners were carried with a few other items of individual choice. These were the basics, but gear varied with individuals and specific missions. Insect repellent, chewing tobacco, and many other things might go into the field. Sometimes, one or two members carried CS (nonlethal disabling) gas grenades along also. The total weight each man packed on his back varied from 80 to 110 pounds.

Supply was often a problem for long-range patrol units because they depended on their equipment from the particular infantry unit they worked for. Some received much better support than others. Suffice it to say that LURPs were usually not as well equipped or supported as Special Forces or SEALs were, even though the missions were often just as dangerous and virtually the same. To send men into dangerous situations without all the equipment and support they needed was wrong, but it happened on a regular basis.

After ten days training together as a team, we received our first mission warning order. I was the new guy on the team, so I was given the job of carrying the PRC-25 radio. We were scheduled to walk out of Lai Khe and recon a several-square-kilometer area outside the base camp.

After we finished the premission briefing, we packed up our gear and prepared to move out. After inspecting the team, Staff Sergeant Ray had us load aboard a deuce-and-a-half truck for the short ride to the outer perimeter. When we arrived there, we were briefed one more time by an artillery lieutenant. Then we moved out into Indian country. It was the real thing, my first exposure to the war. My senses went on full alert.

We moved for a couple of hours before taking our first break. When Ray called a halt, we quickly circled up like the spokes of a wagon wheel, feet meeting at the hub, each man watching the area to his immediate front. We headed out again a short time later and soon discovered a stream where the VC had put out traps to catch fish. Obviously, the enemy was active in this area. We halted once again to drink from the stream and rest while the team leader called in a sitrep (situation report) to convey our find.

As I was scanning the area to my front, I suddenly noticed some bushes moving close by. Out of pure reflex, I raised my weapon, thumbing the safety switch to full auto as the barrel came up. A Viet Cong soldier was preparing to shoot Sergeant Ray, but I fired first. Then everything went crazy. Rifles and automatic weapons opened up all around us. It appeared we had almost walked into an ambush.

We immediately tried to break contact, running and firing behind us. There had been no attempt to run the immediate-action drills we had practiced, because the enemy was already in hot pursuit. Then we realized that they were attempting to flank us and cut us off. It seemed that no matter how fast we ran, the VC kept pace with us. At the first opportunity, we moved into some dense jungle to hide. Ray reported the contact on the radio and called for the gunships and an extraction. He was informed that the aircraft were on the way. We could hear the Viet Cong frantically searching for us, but we stayed put and prayed that our support reached us before the enemy did.

Finally, the gunships arrived, along with our extraction slick. The Cobras began to make firing runs, pinning down the VC and giving us a chance to escape. Once again, we were on the move, running through the jungle and firing at anything that looked suspicious.

Suddenly, we were out of the jungle and in an open field. The five of us broke into a full sprint, and the slick moved in to set down about fifty meters away. Before we could reach it, the ship began taking hits, forcing the pilot to abort the pickup. We watched in horror as the lift ship picked up and banked away from the clearing.

We continued our run into the next wood line, with a large enemy force hot on our tails. The gunships moved in once again and started working out on our pursuers. Their fire was devastating and caused the enemy to break for cover.

We were directed to another nearby PZ, a small clearing in the jungle. We made it to the opening and popped smoke to mark our position. For the second time, the slick pilot maneuvered his ship in to get us. As he sat down, we sprinted for the opening. My feet were pumping as fast as they could go. My equipment and the radio on my back seemed to weigh nothing as massive doses of adrenaline rushed through my veins.

Bullets zinged past us from two directions, but it was too late for us to stop. The VC were on us again, firing AK-47s and SKS semiautomatic carbines from our rear and our right flank. Then, the doorgunners in the waiting slick opened fire with their M-60s. The gunships moved in close and sprayed the areas where the enemy fire was coming from.

That worked! We made it to the slick and leaped aboard at the same instant the aircraft commander began to pull pitch to get out of the clearing. After gaining enough altitude to escape the enemy small-arms fire, the pilot leveled out and headed back toward the base camp.

Suddenly, the realization of what had just happened hit me. There had been no time during the battle to evaluate the situation or my actions. My stomach began to churn, and I felt like I was about to go into shock as fear took over and threatened to shut my systems down.

The team leader grinned and shouted, "Welcome to the team, Goshen!" What we had just been through bore little resemblance to our training. But it had been the real thing!

We landed on the helipad and went back to our company area. The five of us talked before the debrief, then showered and went to grab some chow. I had just experienced my initiation into combat as a LRP. I was sobered by the thought of just how precious life is and of its uncertainty. Eternity was only a heartbeat away.

I went back to my hootch and sat down to gather my thoughts. After a while I wrote:

THE MEN IN THE ARENA

Two gladiators with sword and shield
Locked in an arena of death,
Spectators seated to view the fight,
Gambling on who's the best.
The two valiant warriors begin to joust
Knowing only one will survive;
Always before this had been training,
But now one will certainly die.
Swords clashing, sweat pouring,
Those watching, screaming in delight.
Suddenly a blade hits the mark,
The victim falls into eternity's night!

What are we doing in Vietnam? was often an issue of discussion among us. We were there to stop the Communists from dominating the poor, peasant population. That was what "they" told us, anyway.

We clashed in the arena of jungle warfare, engaged against ants, mosquitoes, snakes, immersion foot, malaria, dysentery, and jungle rot. Rain soaked us as we froze at night. We closed with the enemy as casualties mounted on both sides.

Yet the politicians of both countries fussed over what kind of table they would sit at to discuss this travesty they had started! Back in our hometowns, protesters marched against us and the war, burning the flag that we were dying for halfway around the world. They labeled us "baby killers" and "crazies," as if we were something alien to them.

It seemed a strange situation we found ourselves in. We took ground at such a high price, then gave it back again. We struck the enemy mortal blows, then backed away and let him recover again. Why were we not allowed to win? What were we supposed to think?

Chapter 2

Imagine That!

When new people arrived at their assigned units in Nam, they usually got initiated with not so pleasant duties. Part of that was done to humiliate the new guy a little, to remind him that he was the low man in the pecking order. Likewise, a person had to slowly become acclimated to such a drastic change in the weather. This climate was extremely humid and miserably hot. So filling sandbags was a good way to make one sweat lots of toxins out while adjusting to the tropical heat. I got in on my share of sandbagging.

Another unpleasant duty new guys often found themselves engaged in was to empty the honey buckets from the outhouses. That involved opening a back door from the two-hole outhouse latrine and pulling out the full barrels of excrement. Then, we had to move them back a way. At that point, we poured some diesel on them and struck a match. The smell was atrocious, and it permeated everything. It got in our clothes and made them stink. When we returned from that detail, nobody wanted to be close by. So, it was straight to the shower to try to wash away the pungent aroma. I learned it was good to be kind of unavailable when that duty came around. We called it ghosting. Disappearing was the key. We did not want to get caught in our hootch or messing around the company area; some NCO-type sergeant might volunteer our services.

Another duty that new guys were tapped to pull was

all-night perimeter guard, a really nasty responsibility. We got assigned to a bunker with one or two other guys whom we usually did not know. They might be with a unit on the other side of the camp. We spent the night looking out the bunker at the concertina wire, watching for Charlie to come. Our weapons might include a machine gun or merely our own organic weapons. The hours were very boring and miserable as we squinted through slits in the bunker or peered through a starlight scope. Charlie wasn't the only enemy that might come calling on us while we were on guard. Snakes—mostly poisonous—rats, lizards, ants, mosquitoes, and other bugs called the bunkers home. Sleep was a commodity we could not afford. So, while on perimeter guard, thoughts about home and a multitude of other things channeled through our minds.

As the night crawled on, we would start imagining movement outside the wire not too far from the bunker. Was it real or just our minds and eyes playing tricks on us? Sappers were elite enemy special-operation soldiers who were trained to penetrate perimeters and wreak havoc. They crawled on their stomachs and backs, inching along through the perimeter wire with cunning mastery. Then, when they made it to the bunker lines, they would toss in satchel-charge explosives and begin sabotage and harassment. So we all had no desire to get caught not paying attention; that might shorten one's life span considerably. All night long, we wondered who or what was out there trying to creep up on us. The imagination worked overtime conjuring up forms for our consideration. What was real, and what was not?

My first and only night to pull perimeter guard certainly held me mesmerized. I had a pretty vivid imagination anyway, so I was quite jumpy. Perimeter guard was vastly different from sitting in a deer blind waiting for the big twelve-point buck to show up for the kill. We were really in a war zone, and enemy territory was everywhere. That twelve-point buck might be a twelve-man squad with RPGs (rocket-propelled grenades) and machine guns who would attempt to make us extinct if they caught us not paying attention. I did not like that thought at all, so I concentrated and stayed alert. Morning found me one tired trooper, but nobody had breached my area of responsibility. I had survived another night in Vietnam. Imagine that! I only had 349 or so to go. My tour of duty was going to instill discipline in me and make me more mature, if I lived through it.

Chapter 3

The Buscapade

What was an ordinary Lurp mission? It seemed that none were really ordinary. We had to expect the unexpected. Some missions carried more excitement than others, but the adrenaline flow always came with the insertion. The "X-factor" always tinkered with our imaginations. Sometimes the stress and speculation became real mind benders.

Along with the four teams usually working out of Lai Khe, we had some teams launching out of Di An and Quan Loi. All three base camps were on "Thunder Road," Highway 13.

During the fall of 1968, Team Wildcat 7 got a warning order for a launch out of Quan Loi. The team was comprised of some seasoned men. Charlie Hartsoe was the TL, while Tony Kirby backed him up as the ATL. Greg Bennett carried the radio to handle commo, and Chief Vaughn Isaacs lugged the M-60 machine gun. Rodney Hayashi packed the M-79 grenade launcher. Ron Crews pulled point.

Wildcat 7 went in on a last-light insertion, apparently getting in clean. They lay dog for almost half an hour before moving out. Villages and trails were to be monitored in their AO. The first day proved uneventful, and they had an equally quiet night. The second day resulted in nothing much either, but they covered about five kilometers. Again, night two produced no sightings to report. Likewise, day three found a dry hole. Lots of fresh sign was discovered, but no enemy troops appeared. Day four found the team heading east. After moving a couple of hours, they made a sitrep. TOC gave them orders to change route to a northerly heading, toward Highway 13 and Loc Ninh where, supposedly, VC tax collectors were forming roadblocks and shaking down all Viet civilians who came along. That news brought a little adrenaline rush as boredom had by then set in. But the team had to move maybe five klicks through some very difficult terrain. Time was against them. One option did present itself, a dangerous one. They could cut through a rubber plantation and make much better time—if an ambush didn't get them. Hartsoe asked TOC for suggestions. They instructed him to take the shortcut through the rubber and find the VC roadblock. So, they moved up to the plantation and spread out at appropriate intervals, using the trees for cover when possible. It was very uncomfortable there as the team was quite vulnerable to attack. Finally, they cleared the rubber without incident and moved in on Thunder Road. TOC reported the VC were about two klicks up the road from where they would intersect it.

As they got visual sighting of Highway 13, a Lambretta motor scooter came by, heading south at a slow pace. Hartsoe told three team members to stop it and check out the occupants. As the Lurps approached the Vietnamese, they pointed north, yelling, "VC! Bad VC!"

Suddenly, a bus appeared on the road coming from the south, so Chief pointed the M-60 toward the driver, to get him to stop. The bus screeched to a halt, and Chief ordered everybody to get off except for the driver. Quickly, the team hopped on the bus, with Chief getting on the roof among crates of chickens and some baggage. He got prone, pointing the M-60 down the road in front of them. Hartsoe motioned the driver to move out while they contacted TOC. They reported that Wildcat 7 had commandeered a bus and was commencing to advance toward the bad guys. TOC seemed to be stunned and asked the RTO to repeat the sitrep. A bus certainly made for unique transportation for a special operations team.

As the driver turned around a bend in the road, the road-block was in sight, with twenty or thirty Vietnamese standing around. When the bus approached the group, two guys broke away in a dead run, heading for the jungle. The team dismounted and pursued them, firing on full auto. This seemed to give the VC an extra adrenaline rush as they picked up the pace, finally moving into the woods. The team decided not to pursue any farther as dusk was coming on fast. They surely did not relish getting caught in an ambush. So they did not catch their prey, but they did recover a ruck-sack with maps, money, marijuana, and documents. They picked up some AK-47 ammo and a canteen, too. When the Lurps arrived back at Thunder Road, everyone had disappeared. The bus and people had split. The team called for an extraction and was picked up shortly.

After four hours of downtime, Wildcat 7 got news that it was to be inserted again the very next day, another last-light insertion back into the same AO. Rest was sometimes a wonderful thought, but real opportunities for it were fleeting. So they got more ammo, food, water, and prepared to go in again.

Wildcat 7 inserted on an extremely small LZ that looked too tiny for the slick to get into. However, with the pilot's expert guidance, the ship descended into the opening and deposited the team. The men quickly hopped off and melted into the dense cover.

After they circled up in concealment for a while, all seemed to be normal, so they released the choppers and continued the mission. Crews led them away from the LZ and into the bush. After moving a kilometer, the team came to a high-speed trail that showed plenty of fresh sign. So they walked parallel to it for about one hundred meters before discovering a fork. Hartsoe sent Kirby and Crews on a short recon. They found a spot with good cover and concealment where the team could monitor the fork, watching both paths. So they decided to RON (remain overnight) there. First, they put out claymore antipersonnel mines in case company came. Charlie Hartsoe decided to spend the night on a 50 percent watch; half the men would rest while half observed.

At around 2300 hours, the whole team was alerted to some unusual noises. First, voices came from down the trail. Then noise picked up around them out in the brush. Rapidly, the sounds got closer to the team's position. It seemed to be almost all around them, making for a very uncomfortable situation. Finally, the enemy seemed to be about to walk into the Lurps' perimeter, so they hit the clackers, detonating the claymore mines. An incredible group of explosions erupted almost simultaneously, mowing down jungle and everything in the path of the mines' blast area. Suddenly, the night lit up with green tracers as the enemy AK-47 rifles started their unmistakable popping.

The Lurps wisely lay silent, not returning fire. Bennett made contact with TOC and called for gunship support and extraction. Southeast seemed to be the only avenue to escape, so they all chunked grenades and booked out in that direction. It was about one klick to a PZ where the team could be extracted. Stopping after running maybe two hundred meters, they listened for the enemy. Indeed, the bad guys were pursuing them, so they moved out again. But they could hear the sounds of the gunships coming to their aid. Greg Bennett contacted the guns, informing them the team was moving southeast toward the PZ. He said the enemy was in hot pursuit from the northwest and asked for some gun runs. He explained that the rear security would use a strobe light to mark their position, so the choppers moved in to attack. Two Cobras unleashed rockets and miniguns behind the team, walking them back toward the enemy positions. Fire broke out, lighting up the night with a spectacular disturbance.

As the Lurps approached the pickup zone, the extraction slick made contact. He was two minutes out as the team reached the opening. They circled up to await either the enemy or their ride; it was going to be close. Who would show up first?

Meanwhile, the gunships were dealing out a heavy load of lead and rockets just behind the clearing. The team turned on a strobe light as the slick moved in. He acknowledged seeing it and began to settle down into the clearing. Up the team rose, sprinting for the chopper. They piled in as quickly as possible and the aircraft lifted into the night sky. The guns continued to fire up the area, buzzing around like angry bees.

Back at base camp, some very tired patrollers climbed off the slick, giving a thumbs-up thank-you to the crew. They went in to debrief, finishing just another day on the job. Wow—what a rush it was. Danger seemed a LRP's constant companion. Relief came slowly as the team came down off the adrenaline high. Then, of course, it was about time for another journey into the lion's den! Such was the life known as LRPin'.

Chapter 4

Ant Bush

After our first mission, Top Silva suggested that I might make a good point man, replacing Sergeant Harris, who was just about to finish his tour in country. I had already proven my quickness and shooting prowess out at the range, and I had developed the basic necessary skills of a good point man while growing up as a hunter and woodsman. Since the rest of the team thought I would be good in that position, I agreed to accept the job knowing that I was taking on a heavy responsibility.

The point man was the lead man in the patrol formation. He was responsible for taking the team in the right direction. He had to be able to move quietly while watching for snipers, booby traps, ambushes, and enemy troops, as well as the spiders, snakes, and many other creatures that could place a team in harm's way.

Our next mission was to set up an ambush outside the wire along a well-used trail. The VC seemed to be running weapons and supplies around the Michelin rubber plantation. Division operations wanted us to give them something to worry about.

My first helicopter insertion proved to be a breathtaking experience. We loaded aboard the aircraft, which soon lifted up and moved away from Lai Khe's perimeter. Speeding along at altitude, I sat in the doorway with my feet dangling toward the skids while holding on to part of the stanchion that separated the doorgunner's "hell hole" from the open cabin. One of my teammates grabbed hold of me, and I was not sure if he'd done so to keep me from sliding out, or to keep himself from falling.

The aircraft commander flew like he was born for the job. At times he would bank hard right, turning the helicopter on its side. This maneuver left me facing straight down at the ground. I never understood what kept me from sliding right out of the aircraft. However, it certainly beat any roller-coaster ride I had ever been on. Suddenly, the bird felt like its bottom had just dropped out of the sky, then the aircraft commander leveled out again just above the tops of the trees.

He gave us the word that we were five minutes out, and each of us chambered a round in his weapon. The chopper suddenly dipped to the ground to make a false insertion into a small opening in the trees, a maneuver designed to deceive the enemy as to which LZ we had gone in on. The AC feathered the aircraft down to where it was almost touching the ground; then he took off to do the same thing all over again.

The next one was the real thing. Insertion was one of the most vulnerable times for us and the chopper. For several seconds, we were exposed in the LZ. If the enemy was there waiting for us, we would be hanging in a most precarious position. Many choppers were shot down while inserting men into jungle landing zones.

Our team leader, Staff Sergeant Ray, held up one finger to note that we had one minute until we reached the LZ. I wondered what fate awaited me. My stomach was knotted up in fearful anticipation of what was about to come. The aircraft started to slow down, then flared out about four feet above the ground.

The team leader tapped my shoulder, and I immediately jumped from the skid. I hit the ground running and disappeared into the canopy. Once we were in the tree line, the team formed up in a wagon-wheel perimeter as we hit the deck and prepared to lay dog. The slicks and the gunships were soon out of sight and sound, and we were utterly alone.

We waited silently for fifteen to twenty minutes, watching

and listening for any sign of the enemy. While we waited, Sergeant Ray checked our commo, then called in the current sitrep to the radio-relay site. Satisfied that we could talk to our rear, Sergeant Ray signaled me to head out, and I took point as we moved to our ambush site.

A short time later, we came to the trail where we were supposed to establish a kill zone. There were fresh signs of recent enemy traffic. It was a good place for an ambush, so we started putting out claymore mines parallel to the trail. Once that was done, we moved silently into ambush positions and got situated for what we hoped would be an interesting night.

The sun was almost gone, and the dusk began to shadow us. Then, without warning, my body began to feel as if it were on fire in a thousand places at once. Trying not to yell and compromise our position, I started stripping off my equipment and my clothes. Ants! I was covered in ants—hundreds of big, red ants which were biting me with lust in their hearts. Their attack was like nothing I had ever seen before. By some stroke of basic stupidity or just plain bad judgment, I had managed to sit on a nest of them right in the middle of our ambush positions. Regrettably, they triggered the ambush on me when I invaded their kill zone. After I field-stripped myself naked, some of my teammates helped me remove the ants. It was certainly a revolting development, one that gave me a primary lesson in long-range patrolling.

Later, on another mission, I was on point and walked into a bush full of giant red ants that pounced on me with a vengeance. Once again, they tried to devour my carcass, and I quickly did an impromptu jungle striptease. I had learned my lesson. From that day on, I vowed to become extremely watchful of jungle ants. Not all of our enemies came in the size and shape of human beings.

Chapter 5

The Phantom Factor

A long-range patrol team's lifeline to survival was the PRC-25 radio. Our RTO carried one on his back. Sometimes a second patrol member carried one, but usually one was all we had. When we needed artillery or tactical air support, our radio was the only link to them. So much attention was given to care and maintenance of the PRC-25. And, because of the PRC-25's importance to us, spare batteries were always brought along on missions.

Quick communication often made the difference to a patrol's success or failure, even its survival. Several radios were experimented with, but the PRC-25 was the one most reliable and not too heavy to carry.

One of our teams was given a mission warning order for a recon west of Lai Khe, about a twenty-minute flight out by chopper. So they made all the normal preparations to ready for the launch. My team was on stand-down after being extracted the prior evening, so we were relaxing around the company area.

The team made a clean insertion and called in a sitrep of all clear. They began their mission, regularly communicating with TOC to keep them updated. It was essential to contact the TOC every hour stating their progress and any pertinent information worthy of passing on.

Later, as we were playing football, we heard the TOC was

not getting any commo from the team. Sitreps were vital, and the team had missed two in a row. A chopper was dispatched to fly over the team's last known location, hoping to raise them on the radio. If for some reason the Lurps could not use the radio, it could use a signal mirror or orange panel to signal the ship. Sometimes radios developed problems; other times radio silence was an indication the team was in trouble or even had been destroyed by the enemy. This time the command-and-control chopper had no success in locating the team.

We stopped our game and got our gear together so we could go in as a reaction force if needed, then we gathered around the tactical operations center hoping to get word on our buddies in the bush. Another team was in on stand-down and was prepared to combine with us if a reaction force became necessary.

Usually, if one was available, a 1st Infantry Division aerorifle platoon was used in such situations. But we were not taking any chances. Long-range teams were always ready to go in to rescue one of their own in need.

After the team missed four sitreps, some action was about to begin. The TOC was buzzing with activity. We were finally told that an aerorifle platoon was going to insert. Something needed to happen fast, and we were eager to go take care of our own.

The tension was mounting around the company area. What was going on out there? Were they alive or wounded or lost or, maybe, even prisoners? Our minds were spinning, and we felt very discouraged that we had not already gone in after them.

Suddenly, someone came out of the TOC to inform us that the team had just reported in. Everyone was okay; the team had tried to call in several times before the radio began working. They continued the patrol, and we breathed a sigh of relief.

After the Lurps had returned from the mission, we discussed the scenario. The team did not know what had happened. The radio had checked out okay, and even spare batteries had not helped. We had worked the AO before with no problems with commo. The terrain didn't cause a lot of dead zones, i.e., places where commo would not work. After discussing it for a while, we gave up on solving the mystery. We chalked up the radio silence to "The Phantom Factor!"

Chapter 6

Peace and War

Threatening to wash us all away, the rain cascaded down with unrelenting ferocity. We had just finished a mission and were standing down after debriefing. I lay on my cot inside our hootch, meditating about peace and war. These two words carried many ramifications.

Nations had functioned side by side for many years in neighborly coexistence. Peace allowed each to carry on in its unique way. One strove for industrialization while another chose to live a simpler way of life passed down by former generations.

Suddenly, some disagreement brought the two neighbors on a collision course. Representatives met to try to prevent the potential conflict, but the attempt came to no avail. War broke out, causing pain, heartache, and death. Finally, one nation prevailed in the struggle, but both sides suffered irreparably. And what was really accomplished by it all? How many times had that scenario played itself out? Since the beginning of time, societies seemed to have existed in a love/hate relationship. Maybe this is because individual families have dealt with the same problems as societies have.

A husband and wife made a commitment to love and cherish each other through thick and thin. They bore children and increased their fold. Yes, the peaceful household sometimes became shaken with division, but reconciliation overcame potential fracture of the family. However,

somewhere down the long road of teamwork, a storm cloud
blew in. Mom and Dad changed their feelings and let go of
their commitment. The family disintegrated into individual
shattered lives. It all started with a disagreement, but it
ended in disbandment. Why? Maybe the key lies in the
uniqueness of individuals and their willingness and or ability to live in harmony within themselves as well as with
others.

A person pursued and finally achieved a major objective
and felt on top of the world. He had worked very hard to
climb the ladder of economic success. The years were filled
with harsh lessons and some setbacks. But perseverance had
prevailed, moving him to the top of the class economically.
However, standing on the pinnacle of a deep bank account,
he was so very lonely. He had nobody in his life to share in
the good fortune. His soul became a war zone; his mind was
ravaged with sorrow. Money turned peace into emotional
poverty. So what was the good in the gold once it became
bitter?

We had been transported from our peaceful lives at home
to the far side of the world. Our government told us to go
help the South Vietnamese people gain their freedom from
the Communists so they could live in peace. That sounded
reasonable at first. But, how could we help their military
fight for freedom when they weren't committed to fighting
to keep a free government? Also, our enemies had no bound-
aries placed on them, but we were not allowed to cross into
Cambodia, Laos, or North Vietnam! Peace certainly carried
a heavy price tag, but war constantly assaulted the hope of
achievement.

After considering such a heavy topic, I was brought out of
my reflections by the sounds of war. Big Red One artillery
fire began shaking my hootch and my soul. I got up to go to
mail call. Maybe a letter from home would bring some sol-
ace to my mind, a little peace in the midst of the storm.

Chapter 7

Twin Cobras

When our team was on stand-down between missions, we used the idle time to do some additional training, catch up on lost sleep, and play a little. Our favorite pastime to run off a little stress was something we called caveman basketball. It was played on the court we built in our company area. The backboard and goal were homemade, and the court wasn't in the best of shape, but it worked.

One day, some of the guys were competing in a hotly contested game. In caveman basketball, almost everything was legal; scoring points was the only objective. How the player did so was left up to his imagination. Elbows, tripping, shoving, traveling, even a little hand-to-hand combat could, and often did, occur during a game. However, it was all in the name of fun and relaxation, so no one ever took offense at anything.

While we were engaging in a friendly game one afternoon, the enemy decided to get into the act and lobbed a few 122mm rockets into Lai Khe, something that was really not so uncommon. At first, the rockets were falling on the other side of the base camp so we continued to play. The newbies at the CIC school next door, and the infantry unit on the other side of us, scrambled into their bunkers at the sound of the first explosion. Then, from the safety of their bunkers, they began yelling at us and shouting that LRPs were crazy.

Of course, that did nothing to persuade us to join them in the relative safety of the bunkers; we had to prove to them that we were, indeed, crazy.

Soon the rockets began walking closer to the LRP compound and, reluctantly, we stopped playing to see just how close they would come. Well, they began to get even closer. Unable to keep up our false bravado in the face of the enemy's incoming fire, we began heading slowly in the general direction of our bunkers. By the time the rockets were hitting a hundred fifty meters or so from where we stood, we figured it was about time for us to go underground.

I ran to a bunker that appeared to have been unused since the French had controlled Vietnam. As I got halfway down the steps, I saw that the interior of the bunker was pitch-black. A sudden feeling came over me that something was not right, and I should get out of there quickly. Logic dictated that I should ignore the feeling and take cover in the bunker because of the rockets I could hear outside just beginning to impact in our perimeter. But I ignored that danger, turned around, and started up the steps, almost knocking over another LRP who had followed me down. It was then that we spotted the huge king cobra coming up the steps behind us. Not only was he angry but his mate was right behind him, and she looked more upset than he did.

My fellow LRP and I decided to take our chances with the enemy's rockets, and made like Olympic sprinters as we left the bunker and the cobras behind.

It had been just another dull, uneventful day on standdown. Yet, so many things could happen to you in that exotic country that could injure or kill a man. That fact kept us in a state of constant stress, whether we were in the rear or out on patrol. The only difference was the amount of stress. One had to always be careful and alert to any danger. The simple fact of life was to always expect the unexpected.

We even heard the story of a LRP team from another infantry division that had been attacked by a tiger one dark night.* The team leader was killed by the huge cat. Other teams were attacked by water buffaloes. It paid to stay alert. Vietnam was not a healthy place. Humans, beasts, the land, and even the elements could, and often did, conspire to kill you. Usually, we were happy at the mention of Cobras—that is, the helicopter gunship type; the snake could put a real damper on one's day.

---

* Force Recon Marine Doc Norton gives a documented account of one such attack in his *Force Recon Diary, 1970*, published by Ballantine Books in 1992.

Chapter 8

Red Alert

Each time we launched on a mission, the pressure mounted. The throat got dry, and the familiar knot reappeared in the stomach. Fear manifested itself in myriad ways. Heart palpitations, nausea, dry mouth, irritability, melancholy, and so on, assaulted the team. Some men were very somber and quiet before launching; others became very talkative, jocular, in an attempt to mask or lighten the anxiety.

From the time we received a warning order until we hit the ground, the tension grew. Then, once the insertion took place, things changed. We focused on our mission and functioned as a team. The tension did not subside; it changed dimension: we had no time to think of what *might* happen. What *actually* happened every minute was the focus. We were entirely immersed in the matters at hand. Carrying out the mission successfully and surviving until the next one mattered most.

Being the point man demanded absolute concentration every minute we moved. The entire team depended on me to lead it on the correct course and to do that safely! When we broke for a rest, we sat in a circle with our backs together. Everyone's area of responsibility was straight ahead, which made it not quite so demanding on me. However, when we got up to move out, my mind had to completely orient itself to the immediate situation. If we crossed an open area, I could not lead us into the open field on a straight compass course. My job was to get us around that open area and back on the correct heading safely. Sometimes we took almost an hour to move a mere fifty meters.

We had to adapt to the elements. The terrain changed regularly. We might be traveling on level ground in elephant grass twelve to fifteen feet tall while wading in water ankle-deep. Then we would move into a rice-paddy area that was more open. Later, traveling might become more difficult if, say, we were traversing mountains and/or thick jungle. The variety of terrain determined how quickly or slowly we proceeded. Also, it dictated how close together or far apart each man would be from the next in line. When it rained, because the rain muffled our noise, we moved without as much fear of being heard. On the other hand, rain made it equally difficult for us to hear the enemy.

Most of our patrols were scheduled to be three to five days long, and the intensity of concentration required on a mission and the fact that we got little sleep made each day a little tougher. Not to mention the physical exertion required by our carrying all our equipment and supplies. When extraction time finally came, we were drained, weary, and miserable. We boarded those choppers for base with an exhausting case of what one might call jungle fever.

During the day, we covered a lot of ground, surviving the unmerciful heat that at times reached over 110 degrees Fahrenheit. Sweat soaked our fatigues and coated our bodies, draining us of energy and our strength.

Then at night, in our RON, lying hidden in the densest jungle we could find, the rain would often come down in sheets, leaving us still soaked and miserable. Of course, with the sun gone, the lower temperatures were bone chilling. Lying out there in the jungle at night in the pouring rain hour after hour was just miserable.

The ground fog sometimes rolled in around us specter-like, adding a macabre aura to an already terrifying environment and making it impossible to see. Knowing that we were blind until daylight and that the only friendly element within miles was the other five men hidden in the darkness around me, guaranteed a most unsettling night.

I cringed when I thought of the thousands of mosquitoes buzzing around me, carrying both vivax and falciparum malaria. In addition, there were countless varieties of snakes, insects, and plants out there in the jungle that possessed toxins that could kill or sicken us if we came in contact with them. It was unnerving. Wild water buffaloes, elephants, tigers, leopards, and numerous other wild animals roamed the jungles at night. All of them were potentially dangerous. Then there were the VC and the NVA who could, and would, show up anywhere at anytime, looking to shorten our lives. College didn't seem so boring after all.

That was the last night on patrol; our extraction was scheduled for the next day. If everything went all right, we would be back at Lai Khe by 0900. The rain finally stopped, and the fog began moving out. The jungle creatures immediately began their nocturnal chorus. Insects, night birds, lizards, monkeys, and a multitude of other denizens of the forest joined in the orchestra of sound. Then, suddenly, stars appeared in the sky overhead.

An unknown aircraft flying at high altitude came directly over our position. At that altitude, and flying alone, it had to be a Freedom Bird. Some happy troops were on their way back to the World. They had survived the war and were on their way back to a normal, regular life—or were they? Would my time ever come? Would I be able to put all the war and the jungle behind me? Only time would answer those questions for me. I saw myself chowing down on one of those nice, juicy hamburgers with fries and a malt at Connie's Drive-in. I was sitting in my candy-apple red, '62 Vette. The attractive waitress with the cheerleader legs was hanging back to talk to me as a car full of girls pulled up beside me. It was awesome!

Someone was shaking me awake. Oh no, it was only a dream! The sun was just rising to the east, and the jungle was welcoming another day. It was time to get back to work.

They didn't pay us all that money to dream about food, girls, and hot cars.

We moved out to our PZ, checking it carefully for mechanical surprises and unwanted guests. Assured we were all alone, we radioed the orbiting aircraft that we were ready. We popped smoke, and our ride identified green. We confirmed and waited for his arrival. Gunships zipped by us looking for signs that the enemy had come to join the party. Our slick fluttered into the bomb crater we were using for extraction, and we jumped aboard. The entire pickup took less than ten seconds.

The pilot raised the aircraft away from the crater, then dipped the nose to gain forward airspeed. Reaching transitional lift, the Huey climbed for altitude as it raced toward good old Lai Khe. With the cooler air of high altitude blowing through the open cabin, we breathed a little easier. Surviving another mission placed us closer to our destiny—whatever that might be.

Back at base camp, we finished debriefing and headed for the showers. Afterward, we grabbed some hot chow, then retired to our hootch to read the mail that had accumulated in our absence. As midafternoon approached, the lazy warmth of the sun and my own exhaustion got the best of me, and I fell into a deep sleep on my cot.

I don't know how long I was out, but the sudden blaring of distant sirens, followed by someone shouting something about a ground attack, brought me completely out of my stupor. It was almost midnight, but Lai Khe was buzzing. Sirens, flares, choppers, and troops were combining to make a startling amount of noise. We got up quickly and dressed, putting on our gear and grabbing our weapons. One of our four operational teams was called in for a briefing while the rest of us were told to prepare for perimeter guard duty.

Division intelligence estimated that there were ten thousand enemy soldiers around our perimeter and informed us that an enemy ground attack was imminent. We had yet to experience one of the enemy's infamous ground assaults. Of course, we had already heard the horror stories of how the enemy liked to use women and children as human shields as they swarmed inside the perimeter. Being the courageous young LRPs that we were, such tales only inflamed our passion and resolve to destroy every enemy soldier brave enough and dumb enough to challenge our right to be there.

The team soon returned from the briefing to pick up its gear. As the rest of us were leaving the hootch for guard duty, the departing team informed us that they were to walk out the south gate to recon the perimeter. Headquarters suspected a Viet Cong Main Force division was out there somewhere, and our six-man LRP team was supposed to go out there and find it! That patrol was sheer insanity! LRPs are tough, but they're not stupid; the team decided to walk out to the gate bridge and hide beneath it. That sounded like a pretty good plan to us.

The night wore on, and the enemy failed to attack. Whether that many enemy soldiers were truly there, we never found out, but the alert certainly messed up a good night's sleep for the Big Red One and its LRP company.

Chapter 9

Unwelcome Committee

We were dividing up sides for another friendly football game in our company area. Only one team was out in the bush. However, our team leader, Sgt. Lonnie Ray, waved our team over to his location and told us to get ready for a launch. We went to our hootch and made ready the gear while he took the overflight.

Upon his return, we got together for the briefing. The mission would be a four-day combination recon and ambush patrol out toward the Angel's Wing, close to Cambodia. We added some more ammo and grenades while discussing LZs and PZs.

Early the next morning, we moved to the staging area, the "acid pad," i.e., the chopper pad. Quickly, we loaded into our slick and lifted off prior to dawn. The escort gunships joined us just outside the perimeter as we flew into a new day and another saga of uncertainty.

The air at altitude felt good even though it was already rather warm on the ground. When we got the word that we were about five minutes out, we each chambered a round and mentally saddled up. Lonnie motioned for me to step out on the skid after a false insert, then we flared into the one-ship LZ and unloaded rapidly. I got us into the woods and circled us up into a defensive perimeter. Hearing one rifle shot, we lay there for about twenty-five minutes. Finally, we made a commo check and released the choppers so we could continue the mission.

A hand signal motioned me to move out on point, so off I went on the assigned azimuth. We moved for about thirty minutes in single- and double-canopy jungle until the slack man tapped me on the back and motioned us down.

Word filtered to me that we had company, that rear security had spotted VC on our back trail. It appeared that our insertion was not unnoticed, and the shot had been a signal of warning. TOC decided that we would be pulled and inserted into our alternate LZ, so Ray pointed out a direction and whispered for me to move us to a PZ for extraction.

After breaking bush for about forty minutes or so, we arrived at the pickup point, another one-ship clearing. We checked out the area while setting out a claymore on our back trail. Then we circled up and made another sitrep. When the gunships reported that they were five minutes out and closing, our ride remained another five minutes behind them. The extraction could get very interesting. Who was going to arrive at our location first—the home team or the opposition?

Then we heard the chopper's blades in the distance. What a welcome noise! Suddenly, the guns were over us requesting smoke to identify our location. So I chunked out a green smoke into a tiny clearing. They rogered lime and began firing up our back trail. Then the slick reported that he would be with us in about three minutes so we blew the claymore and prepared to move.

In he came, fluttering down like a huge bumblebee. We jogged out and hopped into the giant bug, and it took off almost straight up. Then, the pilot pointed the nose in the right direction and off we went.

We headed for the alternate insertion point and prepared to launch again. The AC made two false insertions then gave the signal that the third would be real. Just as I started to climb out on the skid, someone pulled me back in and motioned for me to sit down. I was confused until a team member clued me in that our mission had been called off. We were all relieved even though we did not understand why plans had changed; we were thankful to be alive and well. The trip back to Lai Khe was uneventful, just the way we wanted it.

Chapter 10

War Paint

As our team mounted the Huey slick for another mission, the adrenaline rush began again. What adventure awaited us in the foreboding jungle this time? I could only imagine what things had been like back in the Old West during the years of the expanding frontier. Settlers migrating west in covered wagons had to constantly battle the elements and deal with plague, weather, starvation, robbers, and Indians.

The U.S. Cavalry patrolled out of its forts in a valiant effort to cover thousands of square miles of hostile territory most of its men weren't familiar with. Outlaws and Indians roamed the land, looting and killing. In spite of that, frontier towns sprang up everywhere, requiring the enforcement of law and order. Besides the cavalry, marshals and sheriffs were needed to protect the good from the bad and the ugly.

Many incredible tales came out of the Old West, but my fascination remained with the Indians. For centuries they warred against neighboring tribes while maintaining their cultures and living a life that was passed down through generations with little or no change. Then the white man appeared out of nowhere and moved in to take over tribal lands. Conflicts invariably broke out as the two cultures met head-on.

Yes, both Indians and whites had their share of good and bad people, but the resiliency of the Indians fascinated me. Indians fought the modern weapons of the white man by utilizing unconventional tactics. They were masters of stealth, "sneaking and peeking," picking their opportunities to attack, always looking for an edge. They mastered the art of the lightning raid and of the ambush. One characteristic that always struck fear in the hearts of their enemies, especially the white man, was the Indians' use of war paint. When they applied it, that always meant that they were prepared for war.

As I sat in the helicopter with the rest of my teammates, flying over the jungle below, I couldn't help but realize that we, too, were going into combat wearing war paint. The black-and-green greasepaint covering our faces and exposed body parts was primarily worn to make us difficult to spot in the thick vegetation where we carried out our war on the enemy.

Our missions included reconnaissance deep into the sanctuaries of the VC and NVA. We soon became very adept at ambushing their smaller units. We also grabbed an enemy prisoner or two as they moved along infiltration and supply routes, forcing them to remain in larger units; to split up was to run the risk of being heard of no more. We even attempted, though unsuccessfully, to rescue friendly POWs. Unfortunately, the lack of timely intelligence and the enemy's habit of continually moving the POWs made rescue virtually impossible.

We frequently were called upon to launch rescue missions for downed aircraft crewmen. Those missions were always a race to get to the aircrew before the enemy did. We were usually successful. However, sometimes the rescue mission became a recovery mission when we got to the crash site first only to discover that there had been no survivors.

Our teams usually consisted of a point man followed immediately by a slack man who carried a map and a compass and was responsible for keeping the point man on course. The team leader usually walked third in line followed by the RTO (radio telephone operator), the M-79 grenadier, and the rear security man whose job it was to cover the back trail. One of the six patrol members served as the assistant team leader. Everyone trained to walk any position on the team, and each of us needed to know basic medical treatment and radio-communication.

We practiced many different mission scenarios that our team might face out on patrol. We rehearsed immediate-action drills, which determined how we would break contact with the enemy if we were not able to overpower him. These drills had to be carefully planned and flawlessly carried out, or they simply would not work. Combat was the wrong place to screw up, because the price of a mistake there was death.

One immediate-action drill was "contact front," which answered the obvious question, what do you do if the point man makes contact while moving along at the head of the team? The answer? Proceed immediately into a drill called "the Australian peel," developed by the Australian SAS (Special Air Service) in Malaysia. The point man immediately yelled, "Contact front!" to alert the team, and dropped to one knee, opening fire and expending a full magazine. As he ran dry, he turned and sprinted to the rear of the column, while the slack man took a step or two to the left and dropped to one knee before emptying a full magazine toward the point of contact. As he emptied his own weapon, the slack man stepped to the right and followed with the same action as the man in front of him, and so on down the column. The idea was for the patrol to keep up a continual fire into the enemy, keeping them off balance until the entire team reversed itself, retreated back through itself, and was heading at full speed in the opposite direction. When it was done to perfection, it was exciting to watch the peel performed. We practiced it until that was the *only* way we could do it.

This was a very simple explanation for a very technical maneuver performed under life-and-death pressure. A similar drill was used for contacts left, right, and rear. The key was to break contact quickly, heading directly away from the enemy without anyone's being wounded or killed on the team. Sometimes the IADs worked, sometimes they didn't. Each man executing his part of the drill precisely was essential for the success of the drill and the team's survival. If just one man failed to do his part, the chain of fire was broken, and the enemy was given the opportunity to gain fire superiority and begin pursuit.

Many hours of practice were required for a team to become extremely functional. For that reason, splitting up a team or assigning a new member to replace an existing team member was never a good idea; it jeopardized team integrity, and introduced a weak link into what had previously been a strong chain. It didn't matter how good the new man might be; he still didn't know the idiosyncrasies of the team. Familiarity led to trust, loyalty, and better performance, which in turn led to survival. The old adage, "practice makes perfect," was especially true on long-range patrols. New men had to be trained "with" the team as if the entire team had just been put together for the very first time. That was the only way to ensure that they would perform properly together as a team out on patrol.

Unfortunately, we were seldom afforded the luxury of that type of training, which resulted in a number of problems that no one needed to face in the middle of enemy territory. However, orders were orders, and we were given no choice in the matter.

After our insertion on this particular mission, we discovered that our AO was cold; there were few signs of enemy activity, certainly nothing recent. After three days, we made our way to the primary PZ and were extracted without any problems.

Back in the rear, we debriefed, ate, and showered, washing off our war paint until the next warning order.

Chapter 11

Peekaboo

One mission we experienced was quite memorable and somewhat unique. We received a warning order and began checking gear and weapons to make sure all was in order. As the team leader briefed us on his overflight, we decided to carry some more ammo; it was to be an ambush mission northwest of Thunder Road toward Cambodia. After rehearsing, rehashing, and relaxing, it was time for the main event.

We arrived at the chopper pad, but it was vacant. So we sat down and tried to relax and wait for a ride and escort of gunships. The weather was sunny and warm with clouds off toward the AO. After twenty-five or thirty minutes, our slick arrived and set down on the pad. The AC talked to the TL for a minute or two then we got the signal to mount up, so we put our rucks on and climbed aboard our horse. It was a fairly long flight, about twenty-five minutes. The gunship escort joined us shortly after we passed the Lai Khe perimeter. We terrain-hopped at low level part of the way as we drew nearer the target area. The sky turned darker and rain began falling. Five minutes out, we were told to get ready. We locked and loaded, and I moved to the door.

After two fake inserts, we moved toward the LZ, an open area on the side of a hill. I stepped out on the skids and the ship began to flare into the opening. At about four feet off the ground, I jumped out on the rocky ridge and moved off into the single canopy. I circled us up where we waited a while. All seemed normal, and no warning shots were fired. We called in and released the ships.

The team started moving farther up the hill. We finally got close to the crest, making sure not to silhouette our profiles. I wound us around to the far side of the hill, where we found an opening big enough for a one-ship PZ. We made note of it in case we needed to use it later. As we relocated about three-fourths of the way down a hill toward the valley floor, I stepped out on a large, high-speed trail.

Signaling danger, I quickly backed into the jungle. Since it showed recent heavy use, our TL decided we would parallel the trail; we were looking for a good ambush position. Shortly, I came to a bend in the footpath where it headed downward to the valley floor. It was just getting dusk so we decided to put out our claymores at a seventy-five-degree bend in the trail. Being satisfied that we were set up correctly, we called in a sitrep and plotted artillery in case we needed it.

It was extremely dark by the time that we began our shifts of surveillance. I was chosen for the first hour, which passed with no unusual happenings. I woke the next man and made sure that he was fully alert, then I lay back and closed my eyes. Sleep tried to avoid me; my mind kept clicking from one scenario to another about what could happen. Even so, somewhere along the way, I managed to slip off into slumber. I awoke to someone tapping my shoulder. It was midnight, my watch. I rolled over and faced the trail, looking and listening for any sign of Mr. Victor Charles.

After about thirty minutes something very eerie took place—from down in the valley, a fog began rolling toward our position. It was like an unwanted evil presence slipping in among us. I decided to wake the team before it completely invaded our perimeter. We decided to move from a linear ambush position into a tight circle, a "defensive perimeter." The ATL took the clackers to all the claymores.

Within minutes, we were totally engulfed by the fog until I could not even see my hand touching my nose. It was an unsettling condition that made us all feel quite helpless. We could not watch the trail, much less anyone who might be moving along it. So our mission was on hold; even if we had successfully initiated a contact, the aircraft were all grounded due to zero visibility and wouldn't have been able to extract us. The enemy certainly could not see us or anything else. It was a stalemate. Nothing could be accomplished.

Survival was all that seemed to matter as we merely sat close together, hoping no human or beast would stumble over us. We did not dare do much communicating because we were afraid of drawing attention. The RTO made sitreps by breaking squelch. He pressed the handset button and the radio back at our tactical headquarters would buzz. Then, they would do the same to acknowledge us. Using that method kept the rear informed hourly that we were safe. After several hours, we became extremely tense and exhausted. We thought about the clearing up the ridge from us that we had found after inserting. If we could get back to it, a chopper could get in to extract us when the fog cleared. But we had no way of getting oriented in that soup. If our team members got separated from one another, disaster was quite possible, so we waited. Then, just about two hours before dark, the blanket started lifting some. The trail became visible again, but barely.

We communicated with the TOC and were advised to stay there for the night. If the cover lifted enough the next day, they would try to extract us. We were able to see well enough to move back into our linear tactical positions. If the enemy came, we would give them a final peekaboo! So we settled down for a long night. The fog still hung in pockets, but it was bearable. We agreed to use the clearing as a rally point in case we had to escape and evade and got separated. Around 2200 hours, we heard some clanging noises down in the valley. Then quiet settled in again. I finished my second watch without incident and closed my eyes for a little while.

Morning arrived without any enemy sightings. The fog was lifting. About 0900 hours, we pulled in our claymores and headed out. I moved us back up the ridge to search out the clearing for extraction. TOC felt the weather forecast mandated that we get out very quickly. The weather was expected to deteriorate over the next few hours, so we had to get out while choppers could still fly.

Without risking making too much noise, I moved us methodically around to our little PZ. We swept through it, making sure no surprises awaited the extraction. Thankfully, all was clear.

The sound of our ride brought our ears and hearts to attention. We popped smoke, and the chopper identified its color. Then the gunships started working out around the small clearing. Quickly, our rescue ship hovered in, and we beat feet. Once we were all safely on board, the TL signaled the AC to go. The aircraft jumped up in the air and blasted down toward the valley floor, picking up airspeed. Then, we started gaining altitude and headed away from the unfriendly AO. As the strain and stress began to lift from our bodies, deep fatigue overtook us. But we had made it once more.

Chapter 12

Covey of Quail

I'm not sure of the reason, but we believed that LRPs didn't function well if too much time passed between missions. Maybe it was the sudden depressurization that we suffered at the end of a mission. We went from a constant adrenaline high while out in the bush to an extended period of boredom and lassitude back in the rear. Whatever it was, I knew that it was not a healthy situation to flounder around base camp very long. If the period between missions ran for more than five to six days, we seemed drawn to bouts of mischief that we could neither control nor anticipate.

I had become a full-fledged member of Team One and was given the somewhat dubious honor of serving as the team's point man. Our team leader was Don Hildebrandt, who, for obvious reasons, was called "Giant." Despite what I said before, about the difficulty of placing a new man on a team, the teams continually changed as a result of men finishing their tours and going home, taking R & Rs and emergency leaves, assignment to Recondo School (a very demanding Lurp finishing school run by Special Forces in Nha Trang), getting sick, injured, and wounded, or being killed. After spending some valuable time with the rest of the men of Team One, I noticed that we seemed to be functioning well together.

That was true not only while on missions, but also during training and when we were just hanging around base camp. We just naturally seemed to spend most of our time together.

That was beneficial in that it solidified us as a team and helped us to function like a well-oiled machine.

One afternoon, we were sitting outside our hootch, taking it easy. Some of us were drinking while enjoying a smoke, just trying to relax. The bleachers over at the CIC school, where new troops were indoctrinated, was only seventy-five meters or so from our company area. It happened that a bunch of new guys were sitting in the bleachers at that very moment, listening as a briefing was finished by a captain.

During the break between sessions, some of the cherries, aka "new guys," began smarting off at us, shouting that LRPs were nothing but a bunch of crazies for doing what we did. Now, maybe we were a little eccentric; and maybe, just maybe, some of us might have even been a little crazy; but whatever we were, we didn't appreciate outsiders saying so. It was simply something that any LRP worth his Ranger scroll wouldn't tolerate. Without a word, I got up from where I had been sitting and stepped into our hootch. Seconds later, I stepped outside with a CS gas grenade clutched firmly in my hand. Paying no heed to the new guys over at CIC, I nonchalantly resumed my seat.

It didn't take long before the new troops were running their mouths again. Now, I'm not really sure how or why it happened, but seconds later, a fully armed CS grenade got wings and flew over to the CIC crowd, dispersing its awful gas. As it popped and began sending out its fog of nauseous vapors, mass pandemonium unfolded right before our shocked eyes. Like a covey of quail, the packed cherries "flushed" in all directions. Gagging, coughing, and screaming, they quickly dispersed. You might say that we provided them with an impromptu CS-101 class!

Not long after the gas dissipated, a very angry captain stormed into the company area asking for our commanding officer. Lt. Jerry Davis happened to be gone at the time. However, 1st Sgt. Fred Silva stepped out to deal with the angry officer. With his black handlebar mustache and more than three-hundred-pound frame, he presented an imposing figure. He briefly inquired as to the nature of the captain's business in his LRP compound. After listening patiently to the officer's fiery tirade, Top calmly informed the captain that if he was not out of our company area ASAP, he would turn his LRPs loose. A brief but intense staring match ensued.

Suddenly, the flustered officer turned on his heel and departed the area for the friendlier confines of the CIC school. Our first sergeant said nothing to us. We had no idea at the time whether the angry captain would bother to pursue the incident higher up the chain of command, but we were content to allow nature to take its course. LRPs always stuck together, and Top was no exception to that rule. The seasoned old warrior demanded a lot from us, but he also looked out for us and cared about us.

Chapter 13

The Night Stalkers

When we were on stand-down waiting for our next mission, past adventures were often discussed. Some missions that took place before any of us had even arrived in country were still of interest. The following was a prime example of what a few well-trained men could accomplish against a much larger force of enemy troops. Also, it presented some warnings and lessons to be learned by those of us following in their footsteps.

On the fifth day of May 1968, Viet Cong and NVA forces attacked Saigon and 118 other South Vietnamese district and provincial capitals, major cities, and military installations. This marked a sharp resurgence in Communist efforts to carry the war from the borders into the South Vietnamese interior. At least eight NVA regiments along with numerous battalion-size units were operating in or moving toward areas just to the north, northeast, and west of Saigon.

The Lurps of Company F, 52d Infantry, were tasked with screening major bases in the 1st Infantry Division's tactical area of operations. On May 7, teams Wildcat One and Two received warning orders for missions to conduct reconnaissance and to pull ambush patrols outside of Phu Loi, the Big Red One base.

Phu Loi lay on Highway 13 about thirty kilometers northeast of Saigon. It was home base to the division's artillery and armored cavalry, along with others. It was a major complex with great strategic importance.

Wildcat 1 was a four-man team: S. Sgt. Jack Liesure, team leader; Roger Anderson, assistant team leader; Charlie Hartsoe and Chris Ferris. Wildcat 2 was a full six-man team: Sgt. Ronnie Luse, TL; Robert Elsner, ATL; Bill Cohn, Al Coleman, Dave Hill, and John Mills. The two teams were placed under command of 1st Division Artillery headquarters.

Surrounded by villages, vast rice paddies, and rubber plantations, Phu Loi had been the scene of fierce combat during the 1968 Tet Offensive just a few months prior. NVA and VC used the area around Phu Loi as a staging area, a gathering point to strike Saigon and other key targets. On January 31, 1968, Team Wildcat 2, led by Sergeant Luse, exposed an estimated full regiment of NVA and VC attempting a night crossing north of Phu Loi from Dog Leg Village to An My. The Lurp team conducted an artillery attack on the huge unit, which prematurely began the Tet offensive against Phu Loi base camp. After being badly mauled by the artillery directed by the long-range patrollers, the VC and NVA survivors escaped into nearby An My village, where a vicious battle ensued. Elements of the Big Red One's 1st Battalion, 28th Infantry, and the 1st Squadron, 4th Cavalry, engaged the hostile force for a few days, finally dislodging it from the village.

The Lurps' early warning and the subsequent defeat of the enemy was a major blow to the North Vietnamese's plans for the region. Ironically, the Wildcat 2 LRRPs received credit only for discovering the Communist force. The official after-action report entirely omitted the fact that the LRRPs had actually stayed in position, spotting and adjusting artillery and aerial fire on the enemy throughout the night of January 31, 1968. So, 1st Infantry Division G-2 (Intelligence) believed that, because of the renewed attacks and continued pitched battles in and around the capital city of Saigon, the Phu Loi area would again be a transit route for major enemy forces. The Tet Offensive had almost eliminated all Main

Force Viet Cong, so the local "part-time" Viet Cong forces had begun escorting the North Vietnamese Army soldiers through villages and rest areas toward Saigon. Thus, Wildcat 1 and 2 were deployed to find and foil the infiltrators' plans once again. Company F, 52d Infantry LRPs were being used more often to ambush instead of sneaking and peeking. They had become the night stalkers. They were not to take suicidal risks, but opportunities to hit the enemy had become more important than recon patrols. Because there was so much aggressive Communist infiltration close to major allied bases, many of the Lurp missions became short-range patrols.

Wildcat 1 and 2 began the new short-range ambush patrols from Phu Loi, moving out two to five klicks from the base bunker lines and alternating exit points and directions of movement. One patrol started with a daylight truck ride to an ARVN (Army of Republic of Vietnam) base camp about five klicks from Phu Loi, after which the teams patrolled back to Phu Loi at night, which was risky business. Not much of significance happened on the first few patrols. Team 1 even tried a unique tactic, moving silently, close to Dog Leg village and then turning on a transistor radio that blared loud music and leaving it on a rice paddy berm. Hoping to attract a few enemy into their ambush zone, the Lurps backed off and watched with a starlight scope. However, the bait was not taken.

G-2 still believed enemy troops were infiltrating through the rice paddy area in the close proximity of Phu Loi base. So, Team 2 was given a new patrol order. It was to proceed deep into the open rice paddy area between Dog Leg and An My villages to see if lightning might strike twice in the same spot. The team was going to the exact place that Sergeant Luse and Team Two had so successfully worked from back on January 31.

On May 10, Wildcat 2 moved out of Phu Loi just after dark. Wildcat 1 was to be used as a reaction force if the need arose. Team 2 proceeded about three klicks to the Chinese graveyard it had used before. After watching awhile, they crawled over to the same stone grave monument, one that looked like a kind of pagoda structure.

Then they deployed around it with half the team climbing into it. From there, elevated about five feet above the surrounding terrain, they could observe the area. It was an excellent place to watch for enemy forces moving through the night. A starlight scope gave them unrestricted visibility for several hundred yards in every direction. So they began sharing shifts, searching for anything out of the ordinary. They paid particular attention to the north, where the Tet crossing site had been. That was the shortest route between Dog Leg and An My.

At approximately 0100 hours in the morning, business picked up. A squad of enemy was spotted moving into the rice paddies north of the Lurp position. First, they were spotted moving from the east, around Dog Leg village. The TL called in artillery on them, but they escaped southeast, toward the still-unobserved Lurps. Suddenly, the team opened up, first, with its own weapons, and a brief firefight took place before the enemy finally reached the wood line back toward Dog Leg. With Wildcat 2 compromised, it was time for the night stalkers to get out of Dodge. So the team carefully moved back to Phu Loi using frequent two-man ambushes to cover their exit.

Luse radioed Wildcat 1 asking them to meet at the perimeter wire as they entered. They were instructed to bring an ammunition resupply and be prepared for action. By the time the teams made contact just inside the bunker line of Phu Loi, Luse was extremely excited. He told Liesure and Wildcat 1 that they had found the same enemy crossover point that had been encountered in January. After having a conference, the two teams called it a night and got some sleep. Early in the morning on May 11, the two team leaders held a short meeting. It was agreed that the NVA were using the same infiltration route around Phu Loi because the rice paddy crossing area between An My and Dog Leg provided the quickest passage southward, toward Saigon. A plan developed to combine both teams into a ten-man "heavy" team and move to the objective that same night. The Chinese graveyard would be their observation point once again. The combined teams included an M-60 machine gun carried by Elsner. Anderson carried extra belts of ammo for the gun and acted as Elsner's assistant machine gunner. In addition, Anderson carried the LRRPs' only M-14E2 automatic rifle. The rest of the men beefed up with extra ammo, grenades, M-79 grenade launchers, claymore mines, and their M-16 rifles and ammo. That gave them considerable firepower, and they wanted to use it if the situation warranted. Of course, artillery and aircraft would remain the main attack forces, but the LRRPs intended to take direct action if possible.

As night took over the sky, the painted faces slipped from the perimeter, taking a different route from that used the previous night. They carefully wound their way to within three hundred meters of the graveyard, then stopped for a visual scan with the starlight scope. After closely examining the grave monument, they slowly approached it. It was close to 2300 hours as they encircled the monument.

As the rest of the men prepared to place claymore mines out, Sergeant Luse climbed up on the perch to begin observing. But Sergeant Luse quickly whispered to Staff Sergeant Liesure that he had already spotted a column of troops and a truck moving slowly from south to north just inside the tree line adjacent to Dog Leg village. Liesure warned the other team members, then climbed up next to Luse for a look-see.

It was then that they saw a large number of gooks moving westward into the rice paddy toward An My. They traversed the exact same trail as in the earlier encounters in January and May.

The third time was looking as though it was inevitable. Luse called the artillery fire direction center in Phu Loi for a fire mission. He confirmed the grid coordinates and direction to the preplotted concentration, targeting the point where the target trail met the tree line behind Dog Leg.

A number of preplots had been established earlier that day with the division FDC as part of the premission planning.

He explained that the target was enemy troops, in the open, and requested "Victor Tango" (variable-time-fused airburst shells). Then he told them to hold their fire until he signaled. The Lurps began counting troops as the enemy departed the wood line: "ten, twenty, thirty, forty, fifty . . ." until they had counted over a hundred enemy—the equivalent of an infantry company—and more behind them popping out of the trees. The truck was much more recognizable, and it carried a 12.7mm heavy machine gun in its bed. It had begun to leave the tree line, also. The LRRPs hunch had paid off. It was about to become an extremely noisy evening. At least a full enemy battalion (three hundred men or more) chose that night to cross, but they had no clue the painted faces were watching.

With over two hundred enemy in the open rice paddy, Luse asked for a spotting round. It hit just beyond the juncture of the trail and tree line, and Luse called for the next rounds to "drop five zero, and fire for effect." The first five rounds burst like a string of giant firecrackers overhead of the tail of the enemy column. The airbursts exploded downward, showering them with shrapnel.

Then Luse called for "traversing fire," having the artillery fire continuously along the east-west axis of the trail, savaging the entire column. The enemy troops were facedown in the rice paddy with no overhead cover as illumination rounds kept the area lit up and 4.2-inch heavy mortars added to the carnage.

Liesure and Luse alternated adjusting fire onto any groups trying to flee the impact area. The NVA must have known that they were under observed fire, but they seemed to have no idea where the culprits were hidden. The LRRPs' position lay just outside the ring of light being cast by artillery illumination.

Meanwhile, the two team leaders turned artillery fire control over to Elsner and attempted to hit the truck with a couple of LAWs. They missed the target, though. The starlight scope was used to try to aim the LAWs, but the distance and nighttime made it almost impossible. Fortunately, with all the artillery fire taking place, the flight of the LAWs apparently went unnoticed, keeping the LRRPs' position a mystery to the shocked Communist forces. Wildcat 1 and 2 continued to wreak havoc on the helpless NVA as helicopter gunships from 1st Squadron, Fourth Cavalry, arrived, diving like angry hornets on the ground force. Next in line, a "firefly" team arrived to engage the enemy. Firefly was a Huey chopper specially equipped with a powerful xenon searchlight, and its gunship escorts. The guns began blasting the Commies with rockets and machine guns. They reported a large number of bodies in the paddy as they expended their loads and headed back to base.

Taking turns directing fire and watching through starlight scopes, the LRRPs brought in the artillery and mortars again. When troops tried to run, the teams directed a barrage on them to hold the trap shut. At about 0400 hours, the LRRPs heard rockets and mortars firing from behind the eastern wood line, and they immediately warned the FDC that the rounds might be heading for Phu Loi. They gave estimated coordinates and an azimuth to the enemy firing points. After firing some countermortar rounds, the FDC advised the LRRPs that they were ceasing fire to give the artillery and mortar batteries a rest. They would bring in a TOT (time on target) barrage just before dawn. A TOT occurred when multiple batteries were fired in time sequence so all the rounds arrived on target at the same time.

The LRRPs were also informed that they would get some relief by first light, when tanks and ACAVs—tracked armored cavalry vehicles—would come in to help the teams. In addition, an air force FAC (forward air controller) spotter plane would come on station soon to coordinate aircover for the LRRPs.

The team leaders protested the lifting of the artillery fire because that would allow the enemy's surviving forces to escape, giving them the opportunity to regroup, and perhaps pursue the LRRPs. However, they were outvoted and would have to sit tight until dawn when the 1/4 CAV was to arrive.

The FAC arrived shortly and began observing the scene.

Just after first light, he spotted a large enemy force that was moving northeast in the wood line on the opposite side of Dog Leg from the LRRPs' position, but the enemy was too close to the village for the FAC to call in artillery.

Just then, the TOT struck the original crossing, devastating any surviving enemy who might still be there (the LRRPs were relatively sure the enemy had, for the most part, taken away his wounded and dead and their weapons by that time). Liesure asked Phu Loi control if the heavy LRRP team could move out and sweep the battlefield before any more could escape to the tree line. The request was denied, and Liesure was told to hold tight until the Cav arrived. Finally, about an hour after sunrise, the LRRPs heard the ACAVs and tanks moving their way. The LRRPs moved out of the graveyard and joined in a skirmish line with the cavalry troops and armored vehicles. The American force moved north to the crossing point. A few bodies were found, and a few live NVA exchanged fire with the Americans before expiring.

Afterward, the American troops headed eastward through the woods behind Dog Leg, finding some more wounded enemy along the way. Hill spotted one Vietnamese squatting behind a hedgerow and herded him to a waiting helicopter that had been dispatched for prisoner recovery. The lapse in artillery and mortar fire had allowed the enemy to police up many dead and wounded. Now the LRRPs and their small armored escort would have to act as sweeping infantry to have any shot at regaining contact with the badly damaged enemy force.

About a half hour into the sweep, Luse and Mills spotted enemy to the north: one group running toward An My, another troop element heading to Dog Leg. Liesure and Luse decided to break back into two teams and pursue, and Luse placed most of his team on a tank and headed toward An My. Liesure's men took some armor support and swept eastward. The tank commander refused to fire his main gun at the fleeing Vietnamese because they could not clearly identify them as enemy. Frustrated, and fully knowing who they were, the

LRRPs fired their own weapons at the enemy. Unfortunately, the tank had to move slowly so as to not throw a track, which gave the enemy time to escape into the village. So the Americans had to turn back empty-handed. Luse was not happy.

Meanwhile, the lead tank accompanying Liesure's team stopped and reported movement in a small patch of woods to their front. Covered by armored vehicles, Liesure and Anderson jumped from the tank and flanked the area of movement. They spied four NVA who were understandably preoccupied with the armored vehicles. The two LRRPs quickly disposed of the four enemy soldiers. Moving to the right, Elsner dropped two more NVA. At the same time, the armor platoon leader wanted to fire up the clump with a flamethrower, but Liesure asked him to wait until they could search the bodies for weapons and documents for intelligence purposes.

In the meantime, Elsner spotted a small clearing and saw what appeared to be an enemy aid station occupied by wounded or dead NVA. An older soldier seemed to be separated from the rest. Elsner guessed he might be a high-ranking officer. Elsner moved back to Anderson and Liesure and advised them of the situation. Liesure told Anderson to get a medic from the CAV unit to go check out the wounded. Elsner led them all back to the site. Liesure found the older one and shouted out his position.

Suddenly, Anderson heard shots, and Staff Sergeant Liesure was flying backward toward him. Anderson quickly flipped off the safety on his M-14, but before he could get a shot off, found himself spinning like a top, hit in the back and hand. Thinking he was dying, he landed on his right side. Then, realizing that he was still alive, he tried to grab his rifle. But his right hand had been mangled by the enemy volley, so he pulled the rifle into his left hand and emptied the magazine into the brush where the shot had come from. He hit the mark, killing an enemy soldier before he could finish reloading his AK-47. Anderson tried to load another magazine and discovered that his spare ones had been shot up but had probably saved his life by stopping the bullets.

Unable to move due to his wounds, Anderson could only stare at the suspected NVA officer they had originally gone after. The NVA had a pistol and could easily have finished off Roger Anderson. But for some reason, he did not.

At the same time, Ferris ran to the front in support of Liesure, Anderson, and Elsner. When the NVA had let him pass unscathed, Elsner ran back and joined Ferris and Hartsoe. After making sure the shooter who had hit Liesure and Anderson was dead, Elsner provided covering fire while Ferris tried to save Liesure's life. Unfortunately, the team leader had absorbed the brunt of the enemy fire; he could not be saved. After the LRRPs had withdrawn with Liesure and Anderson, the Cav armor fired numerous rounds into the area prior to moving back in and resuming the search for wounded or dead NVA.

By the time the two Wildcat teams linked up again, Liesure and Anderson had already been evacuated by chopper. The teams were devastated by their loss. No amount of tactical success could come close to making up for the loss of teammates. Though additional pockets of enemy dead were found in patches of jungle behind Dog Leg, with an estimate of eighty-eight NVA killed in action, the price had been too high for the LRRPs. Liesure and Anderson were dependable warriors and friends. Having just about finished his tour of duty, Jack Liesure had been scheduled to begin out-processing to go home on May 12. Anderson was serving on an extension of his tour which began in the 1st Battalion, 26th Infantry. So Wildcat 1 had only two surviving members, Charlie Hartsoe and Chris Ferris.

Luse took Hartsoe and Ferris with his team and returned to Phu Loi for debriefing by the division artillery G-2. Afterward, the men went back to their hootch to grieve and discuss the entire ordeal. What could have been a clean sweep for the two teams had been beset by a number of factors beyond their control. Artillery fire discontinued much too early had allowed the NVA time to remove most of their wounded and dead along with weapons and documents. In addition, it had allowed unhurt enemy troops to escape the artillery ambush zone. The lack of regular infantry support was puzzling. Properly used, infantry could have sealed off the battle area, preventing most escapes. Finally, there was no good reason to use LRRPs to conduct a postbattle sweep with just a few armored vehicles, especially since at least an NVA battalion had been engaged.

Evidence that the NVA continued infiltrating the area northeast of Phu Loi came on the evening of May 13. At just past midnight, only ten klicks to the east of the LRRPs' May 11 and 12 action, the 1st Royal Australian Regiment at Fire Support Base Coral was hit with mortars, rockets, and ground attacks by the NVA 275th Infiltration Group. While moving toward Saigon, the enemy force apparently decided the base looked like a good target of opportunity. To them it probably looked to be lightly defended, so they intended to roll through it.

However, after hitting the base with ground attacks, they discovered that Coral was very well defended by elements of a well-trained, seasoned, and heavily armed Australian regiment. The Aussie infantry, along with artillery firing point-blank with beehive rounds, put out a tremendous amount of firepower. Plus, they received additional support from Spooky, a DC-3 gunship circling overhead like a dragon armed with miniguns. A morning sweep of the area on May 13 found fifty-seven dead NVA and a number of individual and crew-served (mortars, machine guns, etc.) weapons.

Though Wildcat Teams 1 and 2 had successfully conducted the artillery ambush throughout the night of May 11 on into the day of May 12 with no infantry support, 1st Infantry Division after-action reports did not even connect the LRRPs with the event. Credit for the attack was given to an infantry unit that had not been within ten kilometers of the action.

Many LRRP operations were classified during that period, which might account for the oversight. But the irony cut very deep when the Lurps learned that several U.S. and allied infantry units were within a half-hour chopper ride of the action as it unfolded. Ten LRRPs and a half-dozen armored vehicles were not a match for a mauled but still very dangerous enemy battalion, but that was all the American forces deployed on the scene. Certainly, to their credit, neither the Lurps nor the cavalry unit backed away from attacking and pursuing a much larger force, and the Wildcat teams had proved again that the enemy no longer ruled after sundown. S. Sgt. Jack Liesure had paid the ultimate price, and the rest of his men paid a sorrowful farewell tribute to a patriot and friend!

Chapter 14

Seeing Is Believing

Sometimes our company was treated like a stepchild. We received missions that were not meant for Lurps. Likewise, at times, after completing a particular mission and being debriefed, we were looked upon as liars; the officers clearly did not believe our reports. The following mission fits both of the above cases.

Team Wildcat 7 was handed a patrol that included walking out of the Phu Loi perimeter about five kilometers to monitor enemy activity between two villages. Charlie Hartsoe was TL and Tony Kirby was ATL. The rest of the team consisted of RTO Greg Bennett; Rodney Hayashi at rear; and Phil Sweeney at point. The five men were good Lurps and followed orders. Of course, the mission was a *short*-range patrol that should have been handled by a 1st Division platoon.

After the warning order and briefing, Wildcat 7 slipped out of the perimeter around 2100 hours, moving toward its destination. The terrain consisted of rice paddies and some scattered brush, that is, essentially open—definitely not conducive to LRPing! Usually, our teams operated beneath jungle canopies containing cover and concealment; open movement brought about an eerie feel. At least it was one of those low-light evenings; even so, the Lurps were still very vulnerable. Lurps needed cover and concealment to work properly and securely.

Eventually, Wildcat 7 arrived at its objective, moving in behind an earthen berm for cover where there was also an excellent view. The team formed a linear observation post with Kirby, Hayashi, Hartsoe, Bennett, and Sweeney lying from left to right. The night crawled by as they took turns on watch.

About 0300 hours, the night sounds suddenly completely shut down. All became silent. Then as everyone was awakened, they heard the distinctive sound of footsteps moving from right to left about ten meters out. Five distinct figures appeared out of the darkness moving past the team's location. The enemy rear security was trailing behind the rest of the group and suddenly stopped directly in front of Bennett and Hartsoe, looking intently in their direction. Maybe he had caught a glint of the radio antenna as he approached to within about three meters of the RTO.

Bennett opened up with his M-14, dropping the enemy immediately. That brought on a hasty firefight, bullets zinging everywhere and grenades throwing shrapnel all around. Bennett keyed the handset to notify TOC and shouted that Wildcat 7 was in contact. He repeated that they were in contact and was rogered by control. He requested that the TOC not illuminate the area. The enemy Wildcat 7 was engaging could have been a point element for a larger force, so the Lurps did not want their positions lit up.

Kirby yelled that something just missed his head and immediately a dull thump was followed by an explosion right at Hartsoe's and Bennett's feet. Surprisingly, nobody was immobilized, but the radio took hits and was dead. Hartsoe ordered the team to fire and maneuver and break contact while heading back toward the Phu Loi perimeter. So laying down suppressive fire, they started to E and E. After moving a while, no more shooting was taking place, so they circled up in a perimeter to listen.

After deciding all was quiet, Bennett checked out the PRC-25 radio. The handset was in two pieces, and the cord was pretty much severed. They replaced the handset but still had no commo. Bad news; they would have to move back into the base camp perimeter without communications, a very dangerous endeavor since no one would be able to alert the perimeter that friendlies were coming home. They mounted up and moved ever so slowly back toward the Phu Loi bunker line.

As if things were not tough enough, a fire mission was in progress outbound from the base camp. Hartsoe had told his Lurps to think of words to yell out to the perimeter guards, so they would not get trigger-happy and mistakenly shoot the Lurps. But the artillery fire made yelling almost impossible to hear. The concussion of the big guns shook the team's bodies and tormented their ears, but they decided to circle up and lay dog until the artillery had subsided. Maybe the guards would be able to hear them yelling things like Joe DiMaggio, Superman, Detroit, cornflakes, Howdy Doody, and whatever else flashed through the Lurps' minds.

Finally, the Redlegs quit firing and things settled down. It was time to try to get in without getting blown away by the perimeter guards. The team moved on in and signaled the bunker line. Fortunately, everyone kept cool and did not fire. The Lurps entered and were escorted to G-2 for debriefing.

What happened next was despicable! Some rear-echelon officer did not believe Wildcat 7's description of what had occurred outside the perimeter. He hinted that if indeed a firefight had taken place, where was the proof? That did not sit well with the team at all, and soon the men were asking themselves why they were sent on ridiculous missions if G-2 would not believe them when they returned.

The team agreed to go back out at first light. Meanwhile, Hartsoe and Bennett were checked over by a medic. Both had shrapnel in their legs and backs, and both were suffering from some hearing loss. They told the medic that he could tend to them later because they had some unfinished business to deal with first. So they went back to the team.

Bennett discovered the radio had taken shrapnel hits and had a hole about the size of a quarter down toward the bottom. He replaced it as the Lurps resupplied themselves. They also discovered that the starlight scope was missing.

So they would have to go back out to look for the scope as well as for the body of the enemy they had killed.

As dawn approached, the team exited the perimeter again, moving back to the previous night's place of contact. Workers were already out in the rice paddies, making the team ever more uneasy; some of them could have been VC or VC sympathizers. Wildcat 7 moved toward the objective very warily.

When they came upon the berm, they began receiving inaccurate sniper fire. Hartsoe called for some gunship support, and that immediately stopped the sniper fire. On the other side of the berm, they spotted the enemy soldier lying on his back with a 9mm pistol in his hand. Inside his rucksack, they found a pith helmet, rice balls, a uniform, currency, maps, and some documents. The guy had not been a VC at all; he was an NVA officer. Then Kirby found the starlight scope that had fallen off the berm into some muddy water.

A slick came in and extracted the team along with the NVA body. They flew back to base and deposited their proof with G-2. Wildcat 7 had made its point and proved their value and integrity. Maybe they should have invited the doubting Thomas on their next patrol.

Chapter 15

Remember the Alamo

Just about the time things seemed to be settling down a little, we received a warning order for another mission. Giant came in to tell us that a 1st Infantry Division firebase was being probed regularly and had almost been overrun. We were to be choppered out to launch a mission from the firebase to recon the immediate area.

We wasted little time getting our equipment together, then went through a team inspection and headed out to the chopper pad to load up.

The flight out to the firebase took twenty or twenty-five minutes. As we touched down on the PSP (Perforated Steel Plating) helipad and exited the aircraft, it was hard to believe that the place had not already been overrun!

The firebase was very small, sitting out in single- and double-canopy jungle. The kill zone surrounding the outer perimeter was no more than thirty to fifty meters wide, so the enemy could move within hand-grenade distance without being observed. There was very little concertina wire stretched around the circular base of the camp, and almost no tanglefoot. A few claymores, flares, and grenade traps were in place, but not enough to slow down a concerted enemy assault. The fighting bunkers were not very deep and had only minimal sandbag protection. There were no more than eighty grunts defending the place, an understrength

71

company at best. The place looked like a death trap to us and left little doubt as to the reason we had been called in.

We dropped our gear and went to report in to the CO (commanding officer). After a short briefing on the situation around the firebase, we decided to waste no time getting out into our element; we had no desire to spend the night inside the perimeter. So just prior to last light, we moved through the wire and across a series of rice paddies into the tall elephant grass on the far side. After traveling no more than a klick from the firebase, we RON'd in some thick brush along the edge of the jungle.

The night was beautiful. I lounged back during my first watch, looking up at the star-studded sky, and thought pleasant thoughts about my loved ones back home. It would be a long time before I would see them again, and there was always the possibility it would be never. When my guard shift came to an end, I was able to lie back and get some much-needed sleep before it was time for my second watch.

At dawn, we were up and on the prowl. I took point and moved the team around to an expansive open area surrounded by thick jungle. We heard a rooster crowing in the distance, not an uncommon occurrence in South Vietnam, where bantam chickens were part of the wildlife. Soon, we heard a hen clucking from the same direction. The birds were probably wild, but there was always the possibility that they were captive birds in a hidden VC base camp. As we moved, the sounds of the birds grew louder.

Moving through unusually thick double canopy, we suddenly found ourselves in the outer perimeter of a huge Viet Cong base camp. Fifty-one-caliber machine guns pointing skyward surrounded the camp. Enemy soldiers were everywhere, going through their daily routines.

We crouched slowly, then froze for a moment before gently backing out of the camp. Amazingly, we were not detected. Once we were safely beyond sight and sound of the enemy encampment, Giant got on the radio and called in our discovery along with the camp's coordinates. We were told to go back up the trail and observe the camp. Giant questioned the wisdom of that decision; it was a job for a major infantry unit, not a six-man reconnaissance team.

But, the job had been given to us, so we cautiously crept back toward the camp. Then I moved us northward for a better look from a different angle. Suddenly, we found an incredibly well-concealed major roadway. Because of its width and obvious frequent use, it certainly was like no trail we had seen before. Again, we backed off to report our find.

It was then that the unthinkable happened: we were told to patrol down that major freeway. I flatly refused to carry out such an irresponsible request. The rest of the team concurred. So Giant called back to report that we would not commit such a suicidal act since we were approximately *thirty meters* from the inhabited enemy base camp. We had done our job; it was time for some major involvement from the infantry and support elements.

Some unknown colonel broke squelch on our radio and told us that we would be court-martialed if we didn't walk back up the trail. After considering our options, we decided to go ahead. I took point and moved up the trail only a short distance when I spotted a VC tunnel complex and a number of bunkers directly in front of us and heard someone speaking over a radio in Vietnamese. We were in *deep* trouble.

All we could do was to turn around and back out the same way we came in. Then, as if we were not already in over our heads, a single VC soldier suddenly appeared around a bend on a side trail and stood facing me less than ten meters away. He carried an AK-47 on his shoulder. In that split second we first observed each other, he grabbed his weapon and began to bring it down to open fire. But I was quicker and cut loose with a long burst, stitching him across the chest.

Then everything went crazy. VC were everywhere. They seemed to be popping up right out of the ground. We turned and began "busting brush" into the jungle as sporadic small-arms fire opened up from behind us as we dashed madly through the trees. The enemy was shooting wildly, hoping to bring one of us down by chance. Panting and gasping for air, we moved into some very dense vegetation a couple hundred meters from the base camp and lay dog as the evening shadows began to settle over the area.

They spread out quickly looking for us, but we managed to remain undetected. We were no more than 150 to 200 meters from the enemy encampment, and they were already saturating the jungle with search parties. There were VC everywhere pursuing, and we could do nothing more than lie still hoping they wouldn't find us. Finally, when the sounds of the search passed us by, we called in a brief, whispered sitrep and gave our coordinates to the command center.

It was nearly dark, and there were no longer any sounds of enemy movement around us, but we knew that there were five hundred to six hundred VC, maybe more, in the neighborhood, and they knew we were sharing their space. We were in double-canopy jungle, and there was no way we could expect a night extraction. A helicopter would have no chance of getting us out, especially with .51-caliber machine guns waiting to blast it out of the sky.

Operations advised us to stay put until dawn. What else was new? Like we had someplace else to go! We were praying that the enemy would not initiate a major search for us during the night. Sometimes, when they knew there was an American reconnaissance team in the vicinity, they would get on line and sweep through the jungle, beating bamboo sticks together to spook the team and keep track of one another. They would also blow whistles and fire shots in hopes of flushing the team. We were in thick, dense, nearly impenetrable cover, but we knew if they wanted us badly enough they would find us—the odds were stacked in their favor.

It was pitch-black and deadly quiet except for the sounds one would expect to hear in a jungle in the middle of the night. Suddenly, artillery rounds were whistling through the night sky and impacting in the vicinity of the VC encampment. For hours, two batteries of 105s pounded the base camp, making life above ground perilous for the enemy.

When the artillery fire finally let up, we heard the sounds of a propeller-driven aircraft approaching. As the plane got closer, it began circling the VC camp. Without warning, Puff the Magic Dragon began spitting out a fiery red stream of death and destruction.

The old C-47 cargo plane had been converted into a flying gun platform. Armed with Gatling guns, Puff could cover every square foot in an area as big as a football field on a single pass. We happened to have ringside seats for the spectacle that was unfolding before us. Through breaks in the overhead canopy, we watched in silent admiration as solid crimson streams belched from the sky and snaked down to rake the enemy positions. Only every fifth round was a tracer, yet the deadly guns put them out so fast that the human eye perceived the fire as an unbroken red line of death. Charlie was certainly feeling the heat that night! Puff's awesome display of firepower continued for a very long time. When he had exhausted his ammo, he banked away to return to his lair.

The artillery once again began firing deadly salvos, pounding the enemy camp mercilessly. None of us got any sleep for the remainder of the night, but we had plenty of time to ponder the coming day. As dawn crept into the dark sky, we prepared to move out once again. Our RTO called operations to give our first sitrep of the day, only to receive some rather shocking news. Instead of moving to a PZ for extraction, we were ordered to return to the enemy base camp and perform a BDA (battle damage assessment). We were outraged at operations' total lack of concern for our safety. Instead of getting us out and sending in an infantry company or two to develop the situation, they expected six of us to walk back into a potential hornet's nest! That was insanity. Were we considered that expendable?

Disobedience would have been the safer course, but death in combat was much quicker and far less painful than facing military justice. I moved out on point back up the trail we had come down the day before. We knew we had to get in and get out quickly or run the risk of not getting out at all. When we reached the large open field of rice paddies, we crossed quickly and moved into the dark and foreboding woods on the other side.

Suddenly, several helicopters flew over the tree line, settled into the open rice paddies, and began inserting an infantry company. We watched in relief as the ships touched down and began disgorging heavily laden troops. At that moment, the VC sprung their ambush. They had been waiting, and had let them come in close before opening fire. In seconds they wrought havoc among the stationary helicopters and the tightly packed troops from the Big Red One. In minutes, the unit had sustained eighty percent casualties.

By then it was midday, and we were still in harm's way. Off in the distance, we heard a faint rumbling sound that grew louder and louder as the minutes passed. This was a new experience for us, and we were not sure what it was. Suddenly, tracked vehicles burst through the brush and emerged in the open on the north side of a huge rice paddy across from our position. It was a friendly armored unit— M-48 tanks plodding along in column formation. We could not tell for sure if they were American or South Vietnamese, but we silently cheered them on as they started down the main trail leading to the enemy base camp, the one where the tunnels and bunkers were located. For the Big Red One grunts lying wounded on the LZ, relief was on the way.

We finally received a call that a slick and escorting gunships were on the way in to extract us. As we popped smoke grenades and tossed them out into the open to mark our LZ, we heard the tanks blasting away in the distance. The enemy was paying in spades for the ambush.

Our pickup went smoothly as the slick took advantage of the distraction provided by the armored unit and swooped in for us. We were soon on our way back to Lai Khe.

As I reflected on that crazy mission, where we were trapped like rats with the enemy all around us, it was easy to understand just how fortunate we were to be alive. In most situations involving small forces like ours fighting against such incredible odds, the smaller unit simply did not survive. Such is the law of combat! The experience gave me a much greater appreciation of what Col. William Travis, Jim Bowie, and Davy Crockett and their valiant compatriots suffered at that little mission in San Antonio nearly 130 years before.

Chapter 16

The Twilight Zone

During a short lull between missions, a few new men filtered into the company. One, in particular, seemed quite edgy and more than a little curious. He took to me for some reason and clung to me like a puppy. I don't remember his name, but he had an endless list of questions. The more I answered, the more he asked.

I couldn't really blame him. Anytime someone becomes involved in something new and totally alien, it's only natural to assume that he is going to experience a certain amount of apprehension and inquisitiveness. He won't likely be satisfied until some of his questions are answered and his fears put to rest. This guy was no different. So I tried easing his mind and did my best to make him feel welcome under the circumstances.

The new man had a battery-powered tape recorder and spent a lot of time taping messages to send back to his parents. He kept begging me to say something to his parents, and for lack of a reason not to, I finally relented. Not really knowing what to say or where to begin, I opened by introducing myself and telling them a little about my family. Then the two of us just conversed for a while as the tape ran. Finally, he shut off the recorder, but then started it up again at what he must have figured were opportune points in our conversation. That went on for several days, and I wondered how much could possibly be said about such an awful place!

I decided to go ahead and play the roll of mentor, since I had obviously already been selected by him. I introduced him around to some of the guys on the other teams working out of Lai Khe, then showed him how to put his equipment together. Even though he was not on my team, it was beginning to appear that I had acquired a shadow.

All of the new men had to go through acclimatization and participated in the PT and the seven-and-a-half-mile runs around the perimeter that were part of our fitness routine. They also spent a lot of time practicing immediate-action drills and learning patrol techniques.

The heat was almost unbearable as we went through our daily routines. Breaking sweat was never a problem in Vietnam! Then, after a four-day stand-down, my team got a warning order for a mission. The new guy's team also received notice. We talked for the tape again that day—more to hide his nervousness than to communicate with his parents. When we finished, I left the hootch to return to my teammates.

We inserted on a recon mission the next day, and for once, everything seemed to go well. We observed some trail junctions for a few days, then got out without any major problems. Back at Lai Khe, we returned to the company area to debrief and drop our gear. After the debriefing, we hit the showers, grabbed a bite to eat, and crashed for a while. We woke a little later and were sitting around relaxing when word came down that the other team was in contact, and the situation was pretty serious. Then the news reached us that my new friend was dead. He had been killed in action on his very first patrol.

Could it really be true? How could this have happened? But it was true. Now all that remained for his family was that stupid tape that we had made. Yet maybe it wasn't so stupid after all. At least his family would have a final, personal message from their loving son.

What were we doing here? At times like these, I couldn't help but question the sanity of being in the war. It was like some bad dream, but much more deadly than any nightmare.

It was almost as if we were in some *Twilight Zone* episode, trapped somewhere between reality and fantasy.

Back home, our country's flag was being burned, and those of us in Vietnam—or just serving in the military— were being mocked by our fellow citizens. People who should have been supporting us were, instead, castigating us and giving aid and comfort to the enemy. Now another American family would mourn the loss of a son, and for what? If I could have made some sense out of the debacle we were involved in, it would have helped to ease my mind. How does one even begin to understand what that war was all about?

We fought and won all the battles, but our president and Congress refused to allow us to win the war. Instead of cheering us, our countrymen jeered us. What more could they expect of us? We left home to go to that foreign soil with mixed emotions. Some of us were drafted, and some of us joined to serve as other Americans have done since our nation's birth.

Sure, the war had its differences from those we'd fought in the past, but "you" sent us and we went. Why were we not allowed to win?

Chapter 17

Mission Impossible

On a particularly miserable sultry and scorching afternoon, we came back from the Vietnamese beer garden after getting a haircut, shave, and massage. Also, we had indulged in some great French fries. Frenchy, alias for Harry Suive, Larry Bourland, and I had managed to slip away from the company area for an hour or so. We called it ghosting. When we had returned, my services were requested.

My team had just received a warning order for a pure recon stroll out beyond Thunder II base. We were to plan on a four-day adventure. So we packed accordingly. Most of our AO had been sprayed about a month before with some kind of defoliant by the air force. What used to be mainly double-canopy jungle had become single- or less. The defoliant had apparently worked. I decided to take an extra quart canteen of water since our recon zone had little in the way of streams to refuel from. We had worked the area once before about two months prior. At that time, it had been a hot area with plenty of VC.

After the overflight was finished, we got a final briefing and discussed the goals of the team and the means we'd use to accomplish them.

We were to go in at first light, which, for some reason, usually meant we'd actually insert midmorning. Upon arriving at the pad, we found our bird and escorts were ready for the launch to begin. So we boarded the slick and exited the northern side of the Lai Khe perimeter.

The AC went up to fairly high altitude, where the air was quite cool and gave us a brief interlude of relief. I wondered how cool the air might be two thousand feet higher, but we would not find out because we soon began to descend slowly.

When we were five minutes out, we each chambered a round and mentally prepared to jump and hump. By then, we were flying "contour," barely missing the tops of the trees. The pilot made a false insert into what looked like a brown barren knoll. Then, we skipped over a hill and sighted our real LZ. Up we flared, then down we fluttered into the dead grassy opening. Out I jumped, followed by the rest of our team. We moved into the trees and formed a circular perimeter to wait. We were utterly exposed because all the greenery had been pretty much done away with. It seemed everything was brown, dry, and quite dead. After about twenty minutes, we established commo and released the birds. I got a heading and moved us out.

It was very difficult. When we stepped out, dead brush and leaves crackled under our weight. We made noise no matter how hard we attempted to be quiet. The jungle was all dried up and decaying. We heard none of the sounds typical of jungle; not a creature was stirring, not even a mouse. We neither heard nor saw any life, plant or animal. What an awful place to be! If that spray killed everything else as it had, why were we being exposed to it? It made us wonder how safe we were. Of course, our government surely would not put us at risk! Would they?

We advanced for two days in that horrible terrain. Not a sign of life anywhere. We felt very vulnerable with no good cover or concealment, but Charlie had fled the scene. Who could blame him? Not even bugs, leeches, or mosquitoes were to be found.

Finally, we broke into some green single-canopy terrain. After midafternoon on day three, we found a trail that showed recent activity, so we monitored it that evening.

However, it was a dry hole. We picked up and moved toward the extraction point on day four about midmorning. Just another humbug mission that we had inherited from operations.

After a couple of hours, we reached the PZ and checked it out. Everything seemed normal as we awaited our ride home. Word came down that our slick was about ten minutes out. We popped smoke as the gunships came on the scene. They made a positive identification on our location and began blasting away just outside our tiny perimeter. In came the Huey like a large grasshopper. It touched down, and we started the sprint to safety. Jumping aboard and firing up the jungle, we took off out of the bush and into a welcome sky.

It had been a "Mission Impossible"; we couldn't find any life when everything was dead. The defoliant sure did the job, but we did not like it one bit. I took an extra-long shower back at Lai Khe. As we showered, the discussion centered on the reasoning behind killing the jungle. Could they do it throughout the entire country? That would leave no land fit for animal or human being. Something seemed terribly wrong with that strategy, but nobody cared what we thought. We were not paid to make those decisions. Higher-up regarded itself as the brain trust; we were just pawns in a deadly game with no second chances allowed. Mistakes sometimes cost whole teams, and that was the bottom line.

Chapter 18

Snake Bit

We were posted for a new mission very close to Lai Khe. It was a little unusual since we were to insert by helicopter into an LZ a few klicks southwest of Lai Khe, then we were to patrol back into the perimeter over a four-day period.

Our mission was a combination reconnaissance/ambush affair. During the day, we were to check out the area for signs of enemy activity; at night we were to attempt to ambush small units moving through the complex trail network in the AO.

In the beginning, the mission began to look like nothing more than a walk in the sun; after the third day, we had found no sign of the enemy. We were tired from lack of sleep and the stress of daytime movement.

During the early afternoon hours of the fourth day, while suffering from intense fatigue, we entered an area choked with elephant grass reaching as high as ten feet. In the grasslands, the heat was unbearable, more stifling than that we had experienced in the jungle because the grass trapped humidity, gave off water vapor, and prevented breezes. The Asian sun was blazing directly on us, slow-cooking our minds and bodies. To make matters worse, we were walking in water that ran from ankle to knee-deep. Then rear security signaled that two VC were following us.

After covering a great distance in the torrid tropical heat,

I finally stopped the team and motioned to Giant to come up to the point. "Hey," I whispered, "how about a break?"

He nodded, and we immediately flopped down, feeling more like ninety-year-olds than young LRPs in the prime of life. Giant took advantage of the opportunity to call in a sitrep to our rear and hoping to bag our little tagalongs, to request gunships to come out and fire up the area behind us.

After lying in the water for a while, Giant suddenly started screaming that a snake had bitten him. Now, you just had to know our fearless team leader to understand why none of us decided to respond at the first sign of alarm. The native Californian had cultivated a rather infamous reputation back at the company area for being somewhat of a prankster. And since most of us at one time or another were guilty of pulling a few stunts of our own, no one took him seriously at first. Cutting up a little now and then enabled us to keep some control over our sanity, even though most outsiders considered us totally insane all of the time. But after Giant continued ranting and raving for someone to come and take a look, it occurred to us that he wasn't fooling around.

"I've been snake bit," he yelled, his eyes wild with fright.

Reluctantly, I crawled over to him to see if he was serious. Sure enough, he was sitting with his pants leg rolled up just above the knee, a half-grin peaking out from behind his motley handlebar mustache. Then a serious expression darkened his features as he pointed to two little fang marks now evident just below his knee. Then he jerked a thumb toward the soggy ground next to him and muttered, "That's the culprit."

On the ground next to him lay a small, dark green snake no more than eight or nine inches long. After the serpent had bitten him, Giant had crushed its head with the butt of his rifle. I dropped to one knee alongside him and quickly applied my bandanna above the wound as a tourniquet. I then grabbed the radio handset and called for a medevac chopper.

Escorting Cobra gunships arrived on the scene and began making gun runs to keep everything under control as the medevac arrived overhead. After the aircraft touched down a few meters away, I carried Giant out to the slick and hopped aboard with him to make sure he made it back to the hospital. The rest of the team would hump back to Lai Khe on foot, since they were only an hour away from the base.

Once we landed and got Giant into the MASH unit, waiting medics quickly placed him on a gurney and wheeled him into the triage area. As one of the doctors there began to check him, I pointed to the fang marks and blurted out, "Doc, the snake bite is here."

Then I reached into the cargo pocket on my fatigue pants and pulled out the dead snake, tossing it on the table. I told him that this was the VC who had done it.

The doctor stepped back with a surprised look on his face. Seconds later, he recovered enough to check out my tourniquet. Then he turned and opened a large book, thumbing through it, clearly searching for something. Suddenly, he turned back to us and pointed at a picture of the snake, an extremely poisonous rootless viper. The doctor hurriedly administered the appropriate antidote to Giant as the nurse ordered me to leave.

Reluctantly, I said my good-byes to Giant and hitched a ride back to the LRP compound. The rest of the team arrived a short time later, and we received information that Giant would be okay, even though the hospital had decided to keep him overnight for observation.

The next day, everything was back to normal in good old III Corps, Republic of South Vietnam. It was a great place to be from—far, far from! Our real enemies could be anywhere—in a tree, behind a bush, down in a tunnel, cleaning our hootches, or just slithering across the ground.

Chapter 19

Wake-up Call

After a few days' stand-down time, another patrol warning order appeared. We were to recon an area around the Song Be (Song means river in Vietnamese), always a hot AO.

While we were en route in the Huey, my mind went back to Hurst, Texas, my home. My brother played Peewee football, while my sister cheered. I used to coach and had a ball doing it. Those were the good times; life was simple. Little things turned out to be very special when you became cognizant of how fragile life really was. Would I love some of Mom's rich, homemade chicken and dumplings and fresh, mouthwatering cinnamon rolls!

Suddenly, we dropped down to flying just above treetop level, and reality snapped me back to the task at hand. We made two false insertions, then prepared for the real deal. My heart pounded as I stepped out on the struts. When we were about five feet off the ground, the team leader tapped me to go. Out we dropped, then hurried into the jungle as the choppers left us behind. After wagon-wheeling up in a defensive perimeter, we waited for about twenty minutes. Everything seemed to be okay, so we released the choppers and began the mission.

I took point and moved us off of a ridge down into a valley. We crossed a well-used trail with no fresh sign, so we continued on. Nothing relevant took place on the first day of the mission, so I led us into some good cover to RON. That night was very cool and clear. The sky sparkled with twinkling stars. We were in single-canopy and had a great view of God's handiwork.

At daybreak, we were already on the move. So far, our sitreps had been quite simple; we had found no sign of the enemy. After moving for a few hours, we started getting into some very difficult terrain. The pace slowed drastically as we encountered wait-a-minute vines, bramble bushes, and extra-thick jungle. The canopy changed to double. We moved for about two hours and decided to take a break. The vines and thorns had torn up my hands, and we were exhausted from fighting them.

After downing some water and checking the map, we continued our trek, hoping to get out of the thickets. We were scratched up and in a cold operating zone. Finally, we made it to a hill and climbed out of the dense underbrush. Finding a suitable observation point, we decided to spend the night. Our water supply was low, and we would have to make it to a stream the next day. After placing our claymores, we settled in as the sun went down. Again, we had a panoramic view of the sky and the horizon.

Artillery rounds exploded in the distance as we took turns eating our LRRP rations. The explosions and the buzzing of the mosquitoes made us feel a million miles from home. We might as well have been. Slowly, the fog encroached into our hideout, which always made me most uncomfortable; I could not see anything. Charlie could have moved right by us without our realizing it. He could even have walked right into our position. Of course, the same phenomenon affected our enemy as it did us. The safest thing to do was merely to stay put and wait for the fog to clear out. But sometimes, that could take a long time.

Daybreak found us still laying dog, engulfed in foggy arms. However, the sun started melting it away like a spoon stirring soup while leaving a vapor trail. We rucked up and moved out very slowly, winding our way to a stream we knew about. Just before noon, we arrived and carefully took turns filling our canteens. We put halazone tablets in to help kill any bad things the water contained. Halazone made the water taste horrible, but it was wet and kept us from dehydrating. I moved us out to some more-dense vegetation. We were back in the heavy ground cover with stickers and thorns. According to the map, we should have been able to break through it before too long.

We cut across another trail as we broke free of the nasty vegetation. That one showed sign of regular use but nothing in the last day or two. We decided to monitor it for a while to see if any company might appear, but about an hour before dark, we pulled in our claymores and moved out; I was to find us a good place to spend the night. (How about Fort Worth, Texas?) We crossed another high-speed trail, one that showed no recent use. We moved out of a valley and climbed partially up a ridge. I spied some boulders where we would have some cover, concealment, and make a good defensive stand if need be. Just after dusk, we moved in and made camp for the night. Once our mines were out, we took turns dining amid the rocks. Then we settled into a long night of uncertainty.

That evening was one of the most unique nights that I spent out in the bush in Vietnam; my nerves were not as on edge as usual, and I actually got some sleep while we were lullabied by the animal kingdom. We heard nothing of the enemy. Fog was seen, but it did not cover us.

At dawn, we moved out on the last leg of our journey. I slowly wound us toward our pickup zone. We advanced into double-canopy with fairly heavy ground cover. We were tired and weary and wanted the humbug mission behind us, but just as I moved us around a small clearing, we encountered another high-speed trail. And it showed signs of recent activity. We quickly crossed it and relocated about twenty meters away. I paralleled the trail until we found a satisfactory location from which to monitor it.

We ran out a few claymores and called in a sitrep. After close to two and one half hours of boredom and fruitless watching, we picked up and continued toward the PZ. I stepped over an old tree that had fallen and pulled a limb back to see. My hair must have stood straight up; I *know* my heart started pounding. About three yards to my front, a VC point man stood, looking my way. He had on black pajamas and carried an AK-47. My peripheral vision caught more movement behind him. Suddenly, we both shifted like old western gunfighters throwing our weapons up to fire. I raked him across the chest while firing full auto. We were in such thick cover that an immediate-action drill wasn't possible. The team merely about-faced, and I became rear security. I finished going through a second magazine as I was running. By then, the enemy element began returning fire. It sounded like a bunch of them opened up at once. As we fled the scene, I popped another magazine in and grabbed a fragmentation grenade. Ungracefully, I pulled the pin and chunked it behind me as I ran for all I was worth. Our RTO called in the contact and got gunships up with our extraction ship. I chucked another frag as we moved into dense cover and circled up. The jungle became very quiet, except for the pounding of the heart that seemed ready to jump out of my body.

Sidewinder, our Australian forward air controller, came on the air. We gave him our location as best we could. He had some F-4 phantoms on line, and we popped smoke at his request. He came right to us and fixed our position, then told us to get down and prepare for an air strike. The jets screamed in at low level, then pulled up and away. Bombs exploded, shaking our teeth and stinging our ears. Then, they made another pass. If they were still following us, the VC were getting plenty of activity. We then moved toward a small clearing that the FAC had spotted. By the time we arrived, we heard the gunships on their way. We had them make gun runs behind us as we prepared for extraction. The RTO told us the slick was five minutes out, so we moved to the edge of the clearing and popped smoke for the extraction ship. The pilot rogered our purple smoke and started to flutter down while the gunships were pouring on firepower and we sprinted to the chopper then jumped aboard. The aircraft commander pulled pitch, and up we vaulted, out of the mouth of the lion again.

As we gained altitude, I sighed and relaxed. Another close call. My mind raced back to the enemy point man I had killed. It could easily have been me instead of him. I wondered if he had a wife and children. He probably had a brother or sister and parents. He would not make it back home to his loved ones, and I had been the one to end his life. Yes, it was either kill or be killed. That is the toll war always exacts. But I saw the VC's face up close, and that made the death seem more personal. Then, again, I thought of *my* family back in Texas. The whole war was insanity at best. Young men barely out of high school were maiming and killing each other. What was being accomplished?

We arrived back at Lai Khe and debriefed. The shower felt good as the sweat and grime washed off, but that face would not leave me. I wanted to pack my gear and go home; the war was changing me into someone I was afraid of. Yes, that mission had been a real wake-up call!

Chapter 20

The Tragic Truth

On November 20, 1968, we inserted four teams into the area known as the Trapezoid. It was a consistently hot area, crawling with enemy troops. Even the adjoining neighborhoods were bad. The notorious Long Nguyen Secret Zone bordered the Trapezoid. Across these special zones, hundreds of VC and NVA regularly walked the well-used trails, infiltrating from Cambodia into areas of III and IV Corps in South Vietnam.

Right after insertion, two of the teams began experiencing problems with communications, so it became necessary to set up a radio-relay site at a nearby firebase. First Sergeant Cook and Staff Sergeant Mattoon decided to handle the situation themselves and flew out to establish the relay station. By the time they landed at the firebase, three of our teams had already been compromised and were in various stages of extraction. One of the patrols was taking heavy fire at its PZ.

The firebase where First Sergeant Cook and Staff Sergeant Mattoon landed was occupied by a six-gun, 105mm artillery battery, an infantry rifle company to pull perimeter security, and a mechanized infantry platoon, consisting of four-deuce (4.2-inch) mortars and two 81mm mortars. As Cook and Mattoon began setting up commo relay, they saw the infantry clearing grass from the perimeter to establish better fields of fire. As the elephant grass was being burned off, the deputy division commander arrived in his helicopter and attempted to land, but the prop wash from his aircraft fanned the flames and sent them racing out of control. Suddenly, the wind shifted, and the fire came racing toward the perimeter. The 105 artillery pieces were already in place with stores of HE, WP, smoke, flare, and fléchette rounds stacked neatly nearby. Now the crews could only watch in horror as the flames quickly overtook the batteries and ignited the grass around the piles of ammunition. The artillerymen scattered in panic as the superheated rounds began to explode. Top Cook and Mattoon jumped inside one of the mechanized vehicles to avoid the shrapnel, yet they managed to maintain contact with the teams in trouble.

All four teams had reported enemy sightings within an hour of insertion. While working in the northern part of the AO, Team 3 got into a brief firefight with fifteen VC, killing one. They were extracted immediately after the battle.

Team 5, working in the central part of the AO, heard a Vietnamese yelling, dogs barking, and chickens cackling. They also spotted three water buffaloes. Suddenly, an entire VC company armed with AK-47s, SKS carbines, and RPD machine guns was moving past their position. They reported their intel and were extracted just after dark.

Team 10 inserted along the Rach Thi Thanh and got into a brief battle with four VC, killing one. They were then picked up and extracted by chopper.

Team 9, working the southern part of the recon zone, initiated contact with an estimated fifteen Viet Cong. It also managed to kill one VC and, like each of the other teams, was extracted shortly afterward.

We had gathered enough intel in a very short period of time to ascertain that the area was still full of enemy troops and was right for a major infantry operation. However, the 1st Infantry Division's operations section apparently failed to believe the reports called in by the four long-range patrols. Instead, it decided to send two more teams to check out the situation. This was nothing more than simple, cut-and-dried abuse and misuse. We were pawns in a deadly game of chess and, clearly, we were expendable.

Staff Sergeant Mattoon tried his best to prevent operations from inserting the two teams, but it was already too late.

Team 4 was dropped into a marshy area in the same AO they had been in the day before. Team 11 choppered into the same area where Team 5 had observed two VC companies the previous day. As Sergeant Washington's Team 11 scrambled out of the chopper and beat feet for the darkened wood line, the enemy, hidden nearby, suddenly opened up. They were firing at the helicopter, and one round went through the Plexiglas in the nose and hit the aircraft commander in the leg. As the Huey tried to rise out of the LZ, it was struck several more times, but managed to struggle back to Lai Khe. A command-and-control helicopter, flying high above, heard the slick commander's frantic cry that the LZ was hot, but when the C & C chopper tried to reach the team on the ground, there was no answer.

Back at Lai Khe, those of us not out on a mission were listening to the action over the main radios in the commo bunker. We did that whenever a team was being inserted, extracted, or was in trouble. We all gathered around and anxiously eavesdropped until we were sure the teams were okay. After all, they were family!

Finally, after what seemed to be an eternity, we heard squelch break and a voice saying, "This is Team 11. Everyone is dead! I'm dying." Then, as quickly as the transmission had come, it was gone. Only silence prevailed.

Later, Private First Class Conyers was dramatically rescued about five hundred meters from Team 11's LZ. He said later that after the team had jumped out of the helicopter the men had moved directly into the trees, not knowing that the helicopter had been hit during the insertion; the noise of the aircraft had drowned out the sounds of the enemy small-arms fire. As they reached cover, Sergeant Washington went down on one knee and began reading his compass and working up the team's location on his map. Suddenly, several RPG (rocket-propelled grenades) rounds exploded among the LRPs, killing or wounding all six men. As the smoke cleared, a platoon of Viet Cong stormed through them, finishing off the survivors. Conyers had been shot once in the chest, then again in the back of the head. The enemy had moved on, leaving him for dead.

Later, with tremendous fortitude and courage, Conyers began crawling until he reached the edge of a rice paddy. Flashing a signal mirror weakly over his head, he was able to attract the attention of another helicopter and effect his rescue. Conyers was the voice on the radio who had reported that everyone was dead and that he, too, was dying.

Then an infantry company combat-assaulted into the area and recovered the remains of the rest of the team, which had been horribly mutilated by the enemy. Conyers had survived, but it didn't help us as we wept through a ceremony featuring five bayoneted rifles, five pairs of jungle boots, and five empty berets. None of us will ever forget that sad occasion!

The tragic truth of the matter was that LRP Team 11 had become the "sacrificial lamb" of high-ranking officers wanting "their" body count, men who didn't have to face the grieving families! Later, a division-level investigation concluded that there was no wrongdoing, that the team was simply "lost" in combat. They had become an "acceptable loss"—a calculated wartime risk.

That incident marked the second loss of one of our teams. Earlier, a team had been inserted into a hot LZ on the "wrong" side of the Cambodian border. As they began moving out, the enemy gave chase. Helicopters vainly attempted to get to them, but were repeatedly shot out. Finally, in a running gun battle, they made it to a medevac aircraft and jumped aboard. As the ship began to lift away from the jungle, it was shot out of the sky, crashing with no survivors. Again, the result of a foul-up at higher command.

Certainly, most of us realized that our work was a bit risky. We had all been volunteers. Many of us were even triple volunteers, having enlisted instead of being drafted; having volunteered for airborne training; having volunteered for service with a long-range patrol company. But we certainly expected to be used and supported properly.

After the loss of Team 11, we began questioning division

tactics as they pertained to us. We also wanted proof that they really cared about us. True, for the Light Brigade, the rule was "Theirs not to reason why, theirs but to do and die." But we Americans were used to questioning authority. We preferred doing and living to doing and dying! For those of us who served in the long-range patrols and on the Ranger teams, we had a creed we subscribed to that had been passed on to us from Rangers of past wars. It read:

Ranger Creed

Recognizing that I volunteered as a Ranger, fully knowing the hazards of my chosen profession, I will always endeavor to uphold the prestige, honor, and high esprit de corps of the Rangers.

Acknowledging the fact that a Ranger is a more elite soldier who arrives at the cutting edge of battle by land, sea, or air, I accept the fact that as a Ranger my country expects me to move further, faster, and fight harder than any other soldier.

Never shall I fail my comrades. I will always keep myself mentally alert, physically strong, and morally straight, and I will shoulder more than my share of the task whatever it may be. One hundred percent and then some.

Gallantly will I show the world that I am a specially selected and well-trained soldier. My courtesy to superior officers, my neatness of dress and care of equipment shall set the example for others to follow.

Energetically will I meet the enemies of my country. I shall defeat them on the field of battle, for I am better trained and will fight with all my might. Surrender is not a Ranger word. I will never leave a fallen comrade to fall into the hands of the enemy and under no circumstances will I ever embarrass my country.

Readily will I display the intestinal fortitude required to fight on to the Ranger objective and complete the mission, though I may be the lone survivor.

RANGERS LEAD THE WAY!

Chapter 21

Roaming the Woods

After losing all of Team 11 except Conyers, our attitudes turned nasty. It was the second team we had lost in a relatively short period of time. Though I couldn't speak for everyone else, many of us felt that both teams had been lost as a result of 1st Infantry Division G-3's blunders. If that was true, we would be some very unhappy campers.

Adding to our anger, the VC had mutilated the bodies of Team 11 after killing them. When the infantry reaction force had found the remains, they, too, were infuriated. It was one thing to be wounded or killed in combat, but to be hacked to pieces and have your body desecrated by the enemy was another thing altogether.

That tragic loss of personnel launched us into the first platoon-size LRP search-and-destroy mission that I knew of at that time. I don't believe the patrol was authorized by the hierarchy of the Big Red One. However, as a lowly enlisted man, I wouldn't have been privy to such information.

S. Sgt. Steve Mattoon, nicknamed "Cahuna," took us on that most unusual excursion into Indian country. Actually, I couldn't say for certain just how many of us went out that day, but it was a platoon-size element of twenty-eight or so LRPs. We left Lai Khe that day with one thing in mind—we intended to seek out, locate, and then wreak havoc among any VC or NVA we encountered.

The basic plan was to patrol as a platoon during daylight,

then split up into ambush teams at night. Sergeant Harris and I would rotate at point while we were moving in platoon formation. For that highly unusual adventure, the team added the extra firepower of an M-60 machine gun.

Loaded up with beaucoup grenades, extra ammo, and nearly two dozen claymores, we launched our mission. Busting brush at point with a platoon-size element behind you was certainly a different experience; it felt good to have the extra firepower, yet noise discipline certainly was not up to the standards we were used to. Five or six LRPs who worked together as a team could be extremely quiet in the field; a platoon of more than two dozen of those same LRPs sounded like a herd of elephants trying to sneak through a room full of broken lightbulbs. At least that was the way it sounded to me.

Moving in platoon formation during the day yielded zero enemy contact. We split up into four teams that night and established ambushes on four different trails. Nothing of any real significance took place that first night.

The next day I was walking at point and moving the team through some very thick bamboo. We had been hard at it all morning, and we were tired and thirsty. Finally, I broke out of the bamboo into some fairly moderate jungle. It was time for a break, which I signaled to Staff Sergeant Mattoon, who gave me the okay. Mattoon, Sergeant Ray, and I plopped down at the edge of the jungle as the rest of the platoon thrashed its way out of the bamboo thicket. All of us were panting and gasping from exhaustion.

I was facing an area that had once been leveled by engineers using Rome plows, large bulldozers. About fifty meters from us, a twelve-foot-wide path had been cleared out of the jungle that looked like it might have at one time been used as a road.

Just as we were beginning to relax a little, like a ghostly apparition, a single VC soldier suddenly appeared, walking cautiously down the cleared lane. My eyes had caught the man's movement and focused on the AK-47 he was carrying, but my mind was not accepting the fact that an enemy soldier was walking across my front.

Forcing myself to snap out of it, I quickly realized that Sergeant Ray was sitting with his back to the VC, and was very vulnerable. Slowly, I raised my M-16 and prepared to fire. The enemy soldier was not looking in our direction, but that could change at any moment.

Out of the corner of my eye, I saw the barrel of another M-16 being raised. Mattoon and I fired almost simultaneously, dropping the VC, but the enemy soldier was still alive and he rolled over into the nearby jungle. Some of us jumped to our feet and began to pursue the wounded man when the silence was shattered by a number of automatic weapons opening fire, a hundred meters down the roadbed. It was only then that we realized that the VC we had fired up had been the point man for maybe a company of Viet Cong who had been following about seventy-five meters behind him.

After a brief but furious skirmish, we called in artillery on the enemy column and managed to break contact. But we knew that they could be tracking us at that very moment, so we retreated back into the dense jungle behind us.

Later that evening, it was decided that we would remain together and form a defensive perimeter in case we were still being followed. Several of us sensed that the VC tried to probe our perimeter during the night, but we were able to avoid initiating contact.

The next day, we scouted around our night perimeter and determined that the enemy soldiers were gone. We moved out a short time later but failed to find anything significant. So we aborted the mission and returned to Lai Khe, tired, but still hostile.

So much for trying our hand at search-and-destroy missions. We were glad to return to team operations, and soon began to wreak heavy casualties on the VC and NVA in the area through the use of successful ambushes and by calling in artillery and tac-air. It was the LRP way, the way that we worked best. Missions were getting hotter all the time and roaming the woods was becoming more costly for the enemy.

Chapter 22

Too Much Pain

We inserted in the Hobo Woods, and I sprinted for cover, where we set up and listened for Charlie. As always, the jungle was its normal hot, unrelenting self. The TL released the choppers and motioned me to move out.

I stepped out on point. After moving for about two hours, we stopped for a break. I refueled with a drink of water and a slice of pound cake. After resting for about thirty minutes, we moved on. My back was hurting down low, where I had injured it in a parachute jump while in Special Forces Training Group. I adjusted my rucksack and marched out, following the direction the TL gave me. We advanced along a fairly flat area and paralleled a stream for some time. Then we approached foothills with very dense ground cover. The pace slowed considerably as I fought the vines and bramble bushes that were grabbing me from all sides. We got tired and hot and took a break in a thicket. Again, my back was throbbing with pain. Finally, I told our TL what was happening. He asked what I wanted to do. I popped a Darvon Compound 65 and drank some water. "Just give me maybe thirty minutes' rest and let me stretch out," I said. We did just that, and my back started to ease up somewhat. One of my team members took my claymores and a canteen from me to ease my load. I gave a thumbs-up, and off we went. The pain was there, but the intensity was not as bad.

Slowly, we covered our recon zone until just before dark.

I walked up to a high-speed trail and signaled danger. We backed away and discussed our options. Our team leader decided that we would find a spot to monitor the trail and put out some mines. We relocated a short distance and found a likely place with good concealment and fair cover. After dusk, we moved into the RON site and put out our claymores. Then we ate and settled in for the night. I took the first watch and slipped off my ruck. My back still hurt, but sitting down helped. Nothing happened during my watch, so I passed security to the next man.

It was a bit chilly, but that was not uncommon in that climate at night. I closed my eyes and slumber came on me. Then someone nudged me and signaled it was my watch again. The jungle was enveloped in a fog as we lay silently; it moved in on us very quickly, and we could not see the trail or one another.

Daylight found the fog lifting a little. After breakfast, we pulled in our claymores, preparing to move. We made a sitrep and waited a little for the fog to dissipate. I got the signal to move out. Trying to get out of the foggy lowland, we began creeping very slowly up a ridgeline. The climbing was difficult on us because of our loads. I came across another major trail and backed away. It was not on the map, so we called in our discovery. Top suggested that we monitor it for a while, and we did. We were not in a good position for an ambush or a possible prisoner snatch. We simply were to watch for traffic, so we did not put out claymores.

After about three hours of observing an empty trail, we moved farther up the ridge. My back started pounding again. Every step hurt my spinal area down low. Then something felt like it popped. I went down in pain. We took a break and discussed the situation, then called the TOC. We were advised to wait for a reply. I took another Darvon Compound 65, but the pain did not subside. We were instructed to look for an LZ where I could be picked up by medevac. So we slowly started moving back down the ridgeline to the valley floor. I finally gave up point because I simply could not concentrate and I did not want to move us into an ambush. So I relocated back to the fifth position, just in front of our rear security which we sometimes referred to as the tail gunner.

We took another break and drank some water. The Darvon had made me nauseated also. I felt as if I had let down my team, but that could not be helped. FAC located a PZ for us just about three hundred meters away. We made our way there and waited for Dustoff to come. Soon, word came in that we would all be extracted. We all were happy at this news. I did not want the team to be compromised by my extraction; I also did not want to leave them one man short either. Soon, we heard the wonderful *whap, whap, whap* of the slick coming to get us.

The gunships moved in on the scene, and we popped smoke. They told us that they saw two columns of smoke, one purple, one green. We told them to fire up the purple because we had thrown out green. Charlie was trying to trick the helicopter into landing by his smoke, where a nasty ambush probably awaited. But it backfired because the gunships blasted away at the VC smoke on the other side of the PZ. Then the Dustoff flared in and picked us up without a hitch. We got out of Dodge City without taking any fire.

Back at MASH in Lai Khe, I was examined and diagnosed with lower lumbar back strain. I got a shot and some pills along with two days' bed rest. I was released, and I arrived back at TOC as the team finished debriefing. I was told to take it easy, so we all showered and hit the rack.

After two days, I was feeling okay. I decided to test my back on the seven-plus-mile run around base. It felt pretty good, so I got myself cleared for duty. I was back with the team and the task at hand in a land where, in one form or another, there was always too much pain! Pain was just a common happening in Vietnam. Physical, mental, emotional, and spiritual hurting was vintage Vietnam. It went with the job.

Chapter 23

Tropical Menagerie

Many people back home wanted to know what was really happening in Vietnam. They realized that what they were viewing on television was only the partial truth. The media was so obviously biased that it often distorted reality. It didn't take a genius to realize that and begin to question our conduct of the war.

I couldn't speak for everyone else, but my perspective of the Vietnam War was that Vietnam was a country with a history of unrest. Skirmishes, rebellions, and wars had plagued the country and its people for centuries; its culture was in a shambles; its major religions vied constantly for influence and power; different ethnic groups struggled for recognition and human rights; and corruption ran rampant, from the highest national leadership all the way down to the provinces and districts. Only at village level did there seem to be some type of order, some type of sense to it all, and it was at that level that both the South Vietnamese government and the Viet Cong made their strongest efforts to disrupt and destroy the lives of the people.

However, the United States of America had decided to become involved on behalf of the "democratic" government of South Vietnam. What had begun as an advisory role had escalated into America's taking a leading role in a conflict. We were doing the bulk of the fighting on behalf of the Republic of Vietnam. We had chosen to defeat communism there,

Left to right, standing: Wenzel, Blankenship, Johnson, Levine, and Flores. Squatting: Goshen and Rincon. Lai Khe, Vietnam. December 1968. (Author's collection)

Author's first mission. Left to right: Goshen, Ray, Harris, Curtis, and Roossien. Lai Khe, October 1968. (Author's collection)

Left to right: Cottrell, Tommy Nobis of the Atlanta Falcons (in black shirt and cap), Dan Reeves of the Dallas Cowboys (in white shirt and cap), Bill Goshen, and Al Atkinson of the New York Jets (in cap on far right). Lai Khe, December 1968. (Author's collection)

A slick extracting Dave Flores and team in early 1969. (Author's collection)

Dustoff to the rescue! Medical evacuation of a wounded man, early 1969. (Author's collection)

Four amigos posing for grins. Left to right: Blankenship, Hayashi, Arenas, and Flores. (Author's collection)

(below) Author Bill Goshen on Nha Trang beach after the qualifying swim phase of Recondo School, around Christmas 1969. (Author's collection)

Class R-13-69 of Recondo School after finishing sea-infiltration raft training. From Company F, 52d Infantry (LRP) are Harry Suive (first row, second from left); Bill Goshen (second row, center); and Roberto Rodrigues (last row, sixth from left). Not seen is Kenneth Whiting. Christmas 1969. (Author's collection)

A Korean Rock Army trooper, Bill Goshen, and a Korean Marine after a boat exercise at Recondo School. (Author's collection)

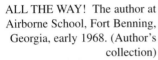

ALL THE WAY! The author at Airborne School, Fort Benning, Georgia, early 1968. (Author's collection)

Don "Giant" Hildebrandt in the LRP compound at Lai Khe, November 1968. (Author's collection)

Bob Roossien (left, with two unknown men), around February 1969. (Author's collection)

Sign in our company compound: Charlie beware—LURPs are here. (Author's collection)

Team One hootch—our home away from home—LRP compound on Thunder Road, Highway 13, Lai Khe. (Author's collection)

Double trouble. Bill Goshen and Ron Crews groovin' on a sunny afternoon, around late November 1968. (Author's collection)

1st Lt. Jerry Davis, company executive officer and part-time company commander, in the LRP compound, Lai Khe base camp, 1968. (Photo courtesy of Jerry Davis)

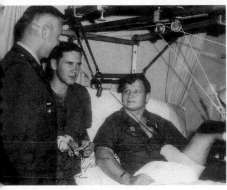

General Moncrief, Larry Wenzel, and Bill Goshen. The general awards Bill the Silver Star at BAMC Hospital, Fort Sam Houston, Texas, 1969. (Author's collection)

Etchings from the traveling Vietnam War memorial. These men from Team Victim Eight were killed in action on February 27, 1969: Cruz, Johnson, Levine, and Liebnitz. Wenzel and Goshen were the only survivors. (Author's collection)

Left to right: Cottrell, Hildebrandt, Suive, Maynard, Hayashi, Cruz, and an unidentified LRP at Lai Khe base camp. (Author's collection)

Hot fun in the summertime. SVN somewhere on long-range patrol. (Author's collection)

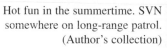

Members of I Company (LRP) preparing their maps for a mission. (Author's collection)

Giant and Flores in Jeep; Arenas, Maynard, Cottrell, and others in the LRP compound. September 1968. (Author's collection)

Sergeant First Class Tapia preparing for a memorial service in memory of our fallen brothers KIA. Conyers was the only survivor of the November 1968 mission. (Author's collection)

Unidentified person and Bill "Tex" Powell (right) in early 1969. (Author's collection)

An unidentified LRP,
J. C. Green, and Larry
Bourland in our compound
around mid-December 1968.
(Author's collection)

Robert D. "Bob" Law was killed in
action on February 22, 1969. He was
awarded the Medal of Honor for
sacrificing his life to save his team.
Some gave all! (Author's collection)

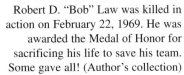

Bill Goshen wearing his cool
rays. December 1968. (Author's
collection)

(below) Preparing for a mission. Left to right: Gramps, Staff Sergeant
Mattoon, Arenas, Arnold, and Cottrell. Lai Khe, November 1968.
(Author's collection)

1st Lt. Jerry Davis (sitting, without shirt) watching over his animals as they relax a little. (Author's collection)

(left) This was our combat shoulder patch showing that we were Airborne LRRPs, working for the Big Red One—the 1st Infantry Division. (Author's collection)

(right) The incredibly hard-to-earn Recondo patch was awarded after completing three weeks of cruel, grueling torture at the hands of Special Forces in Nha Trang. Bill Goshen graduated in class R-13-69. (Author's collection)

(below) A group picture of several of us who served in Company F, 52d Infantry (LRP) and I Company 75th Infantry (Ranger). We are standing at the newly dedicated Ranger Memorial. Fort Benning, Georgia. Hooah! (Author's collection)

and by the time I had reached Vietnam, our commitment to that goal was total. Our mission, as noble as it may sound, was to stop the communist aggression in South Vietnam and allow the people of that country self-determination.

How bad were the Viet Cong and North Vietnamese forces to the civilians caught up in the war? The atrocities perpetrated on the South Vietnamese people were terrible. The simple peasants wanted nothing more than to be left alone. They were content with living their entire lives within a few miles of their villages, scratching out a meager but sufficient living off the land, and being left to practice the religions of their ancestors. Anything else was beyond their interest. It was into that environment that the Viet Cong and their NVA allies came to rape, murder, kidnap, torture, conscript, and pillage.

You might be able to understand it better if you could picture the following scenario happening in America. All of our teachers, preachers, mayors, congressmen, senators, and community leaders would be targeted for assassination. Their families would be killed or kidnapped, never to be seen again. Martial law would be put into effect. Citizens would not be able to leave the house after dark without running the risk of being killed by either one side or the other. Your younger brothers and friends would be conscripted into military service for an indefinite period of time, by either side, on a basis of first come, first call. Your individual freedoms would disappear overnight. You would lose your right to speak freely, assemble in groups, or travel anywhere you wanted to go. Foreign armies would invade your land, soldiers who could not speak your language or respect your culture. Education and employment opportunities—outside the military—would be seriously curtailed, and where you lived would be dictated by the government.

It should be pretty obvious that, under those circumstances, we would no longer be the home of the brave, the land of the free.

I never claimed to know a lot about politics; politics was just something I always took for granted. But I was greatly puzzled by two things that kept cropping up over and over again. Why were so many citizens back home giving us such a bad time for what *we* were doing in Vietnam? We were only trying to help people to be free. *We* were not killing babies and women, the way they kept saying. We were simply trying to accomplish our mission and stay alive in the attempt. Why were our fellow Americans supporting the enemy? Should they not be supporting, encouraging, and praying for us?

Sure, *some* innocent people were killed and maimed over there, and by us. Bullets, shrapnel, bombs, and booby traps were impartial about whom they maimed and killed. Daily, we faced men and women, and sometimes even kids, who were trying to kill us. As much as no one wants to admit it's true, civilians do get hurt in a war, no matter what precautions are taken.

Do you understand my confusion?

I also could not understand our superiors and the tactical strategies they employed. It looked to me as if they had no intentions of winning the war. With all the sophisticated weapons in our national arsenal, you would think that we would be able to humble Hanoi and end the travesty rapidly. Hanoi could have been humbled very quickly if the leadership had only let us cross the fence. The enemy attacked us with impunity from Cambodia, Laos, and North Vietnam. Cambodia and Laos were supposed to be neutral, but they were nothing more than sanctuaries and launch points for the Viet Cong, the NVA, the Khmer Rouge, and the Pathet Lao. Every time we chased them back across the border, *we* had to stop. What type of game plan was that? Our own president and our own Congress had seemingly stacked the deck against us.

We could be home, going to college and getting on with our lives, instead of being over there fighting and dying. We were losing opportunities at starting families and becoming productive civilians. Instead we had become nothing more than bit players in an expensive horror movie that didn't seem to have an ending.

Chapter 24

Bombs Away

It was November 1968, and I had been a LRP for an entire month. We got a warning order for a twelve-man hunter/killer mission to be conducted in an area known as the Trapezoid. It was to be a first-light insertion followed by a four-day patrol down to the Saigon River. S. Sgt. Steve Mattoon would be in command of the excursion and we would be bringing along a pair of M-60 machine guns.

After the briefing was over, we got our gear together and went through a final equipment inspection, then headed out to the chopper pad. It wasn't long before a pair of slicks arrived with the gunship escorts. We climbed aboard and were off into the still-darkened, early morning sky.

The cool breeze felt wonderful flying at an altitude. From three thousand feet up, things always seemed calm and peaceful down in the jungle below; it was hard to believe a war was going on down there. But we knew that Charlie would be up early, having his breakfast. Would he be surprised if he knew that we were coming to visit him!

The crew chief let us know that our AO was coming up. Without being instructed to do so, we pulled back the charging handles on our weapons and locked and loaded a round in the chamber. That ever-present knot began forming in the pit of my stomach, and my mouth was suddenly dry. Before I realized it, the Hueys had settled down on the LZ, and we were off and running for the trees.

When we reached the woods, we formed up into a tight defensive perimeter to watch and listen. Everyone was alert and ready for whatever might happen. Silence prevailed as we continued to wait. Soon the normal, everyday sounds of the jungle returned, and our team leader got on the radio to call in a sitrep and release the choppers. We then moved out quickly to put as much distance as possible between ourselves and the LZ.

Nothing eventful took place during the first few days as we patrolled cautiously through the AO. Finally, we reached the river and began monitoring it for enemy boat traffic. Then, just before dark, a Cobra gunship flying patrol along the shoreline spotted us hidden in the dense brush along the river. Before we could establish contact, he turned back around and began to make a gun run on our position. We were in a free-fire zone, and he mistook us for the enemy. We looked on horrified as he opened fire. Miraculously, he failed to hit any of us, then someone managed to get in touch with the pilot and call him off, keeping him from making a second pass. The only casualty was one of our M-16s, which took a round through the stock but was still functional.

Our hearts were still pounding in our chests as we tried to recover from what could have been a major catastrophe. Still shaken, we moved to another location and set up a new observation point. It was our last night on the river, and we soon spotted several sampans moving downstream. We reported our sightings to operations, and they advised us not to engage. However, we called in all the pertinent information we could gather as the sampans passed our perimeter.

The next morning, we were told that our mission had been extended one day because there were no choppers available to extract us. We were out of food and very low on water, so that didn't come as very good news. Twelve very unhappy LRPs remained on the river the rest of that day and night, thinking about cheeseburgers, French fries, milk shakes, and ice-cold Cokes.

The next morning operations contacted us again and informed us that a three-plane B-52 Arc Light was going in across the river from us. That was the good news! The bad news was that it was going to impact about five hundred meters from where we were currently hiding. The margin of safety for an Arc Light was three thousand meters, so you can imagine our joy at hearing we were about to have an encounter of the "close" kind. To make matters even worse, we were told that the strike would be made in about five minutes. That meant that the option of putting some distance between us and the strike zone was limited to how fast and how far we could move in four-plus minutes. We elected to stay where we were and hope for the best.

What kind of insanity was this? Were they trying to kill us? Why had they not given us time to pull out to the zone of safety? Unfortunately, there was no time to seek the answers.

We got down as low as we could and waited. Minutes later, the far side of the river erupted violently. Smoke and flames billowed high into the sky as parts of trees, rocks, dirt, and shrapnel began raining down from above. The shock wave hit us and bounced us off the ground like rag dolls, sucking the breath from our lungs.

When things began to return to normal, our ears were ringing from the concussion of the blasts. Across the river a cloud of black smoke and dust rose up nearly a mile. As it slowly began to settle back to earth, we could begin to see the extent of the damages. The thick jungle on the far side of the river had taken on the stark, barren look of a moonscape.

Staff Sergeant Mattoon was looking at the scene through his binoculars when suddenly he reached for the radio and reported that he had enemy troops in the open. They were heading toward the river and us, perhaps a hundred to a hundred fifty VC coming at us. They were staggering and appeared to be confused and dazed.

As we observed them, friendly artillery began to pound the enemy soldiers. Orange fireballs began to explode among them, vaporizing some, and blowing others apart. It was a horrible scene to watch.

Then a pair of F-4 Phantom fighter/bombers arrived on the scene. We marked our positions with orange panels for the accompanying FAC pilot and gave him a compass reading to the enemy from our position.

The F-4s came in right over us, flying so low that we could see the pilots sitting in their cockpits. We watched as they pulled up, dropping ordnance on the bewildered Viet Cong. They banked around and came in on a second pass, firing 20mm cannons. The VC were having a very bad day, and that final attack just about finished them. It was a frightful sight.

We heard a deep, throaty rumbling to our rear. Suddenly, an M-60 tank broke through the jungle and lumbered toward us. We carefully signaled him, making sure that he didn't mistake us for the enemy. He acknowledged our signal and came to a halt almost on top of us. Then his .50-caliber machine gun began blasting away, firing directly over our heads. We took the hint and promptly rolled out of the way, just as he began firing his main cannon.

Soon, a Big Red One infantry platoon was inserted on the far side of the river to mop up any stragglers. There didn't appear to be any.

Before the extraction aircraft arrived, we decided to do something about our thirst. Out of desperation, we found a nearby bomb crater that contained a pool of turquoise-colored liquid. Thirst won out over discretion, and we were soon helping ourselves. The taste was vile indeed, but when you got thirsty enough, a drink of water was a drink of water!

Later that morning, two Hueys arrived on the scene and picked us up, and we flew back to Lai Khe. Our team was credited with eighty-six enemy KIAs. The infantry platoon reported that there were blood trails everywhere, indicating that other bodies and a large number of wounded had been dragged away.

Chalk up another successful patrol. Needless to say, every

man on the team had certainly developed a very high respect for bombs and artillery. And Charlie got a valuable lesson, too: no matter where or how well he hid, he was still not safe. The men with the painted faces would still find him and change his plans permanently.

Chapter 25

Bits 'n' Pieces

Gear in hand, we left our tent preparing to be inserted on another voyage into Chuck's neighborhood. Our departures always seemed a little like a dream; logic did not dictate six men boarding a helicopter and being flown into a totally hostile environment with hundreds, perhaps thousands, of enemy soldiers waiting for them! But that was our job, so we did it.

We mounted the slick; Lai Khe was left behind, and the jungle became our backdrop. The engine and blade noise kept us pretty much quiet because we had to shout at one another whenever we felt the need for verbal communication.

I remembered rabbit and squirrel hunting on the Arkansas River when I was very young. Dad and I would kill a mess of swamp rabbits and squirrels. That was so much fun, but the next part was not. We would then have to gut and dress the game so it could be cooked. Then we feasted on a wonderful meal. I learned a great deal out in the woods as I was growing up, but hunting people was a different scenario. We often ended up *being* hunted and having to run for our lives. Rabbits and squirrels and deer did not shoot back; Viet Cong and North Vietnamese Army troops would ruin your day if you were caught out on their turf. We went back and forth from hunter to hunted on most every mission. I did not like playing cat and mouse; shooting human beings was not an enjoyable sport. It seemed so ridiculous to be settling differences with weapons of destruction. It was like two men with dueling pistols. Why not work out our differences at the bargaining table? But life was not always that easy.

We had fallen to low-level contour flying almost to our insertion LZ. The team leader gave us the word, and making sure our weapons were on safe, we each chambered a round. Out on the skid, I stood as we flared into our elephant grass insertion point. About two feet above the grass, the chopper became stationary just long enough for us to jump. It left us quickly as we hurtled approximately twelve feet to the ground. We all hit hard, but everyone seemed okay. I took point and led us about two hundred meters to the foothills. We moved out of the elephant grass and circled up to listen. Two rifle shots sounded back out in the tall grass we had been in. Most likely, they were signal shots from an LZ watcher who was probably letting his friends know someone had landed.

After about fifteen more minutes, we called in all clear and released the choppers. It was time to "Charlie Mike"—continue the mission. I moved us up a draw, then into some fairly thick double-canopy terrain. Rain began falling as we moved through the recon zone. My slack man tapped me and motioned me down. We stopped and circled up. Rear security told us he thought he heard somebody on our tail. The TL gave me a direction and off I went. We moved toward a possible pickup zone. The RTO called in a sitrep, notifying TOC we had been compromised.

After about three hundred meters, we encountered some bamboo and elected to reroute around it instead of going through. Finally, we took a break and circled up. Another signal shot rang out behind us. We definitely seemed to have people pursuing us. TOC told us to advance to our PZ and prepare for extraction. By then we could hear movement not too far behind us, so I stepped out in a hurry. We made it to the clearing we were to be extracted from, and I moved us around to the far side of the open spot, then we gave another sitrep.

The TOC relayed to us that our gunships and extraction

ship were en route. We contacted them and found that they were about twelve minutes away and closing. We put out a few claymores and hid in some thick cover just off the clearing. It was going to be a close call; all we could do was wait. Then, off in the distance, came that familiar sound of the gunships moving in on our position. We gave them our location and where we felt the enemy would be. They asked us to signal them with smoke. We suggested that we flash a mirror instead. Just in case we had given him the temporary slip, we did not want Charlie to know our location. As the guns came over, I flashed a mirror at them hoping that they would pick up its reflection.

They acknowledged seeing it and told us to get down. They began blasting around us with miniguns. Then they fired rockets on the other side of the LZ, on our back trail. Charlie was probably getting some unwanted attention. Our slick came in as we blew our claymores then sprinted out and jumped on the chopper, and up we went. The doorgunners were blasting away with their M-60s, and we joined in on rock 'n' roll (full-automatic fire) with our own weapons.

Once again we had been snatched from Charlie's unwelcome embrace. Shouting joyously to one another in the wind of the ship's passage, we started to come down slowly from the adrenaline rush while we headed back to good old Lai Khe. After touching down on the chopper pad, we debriefed and hit the showers. It felt good to be home. Well, sort of home!

Our cozy tent with folding cots was certainly not like having our own rooms with queen-size beds. However, the tents sure beat lying out in the bushes on bare ground with rocks and roots for mattresses. Plus, an occasional rat in the tent was not nearly as bad as lying on the ground with ferocious ants, leeches, biting bugs, poisonous snakes, tigers, monkeys, water buffalo, elephants, and many other creatures of cold comfort!

Putting up with that eight-inch howitzer about eighty meters from our hootch was not amusing either. Having our cots jump a foot off the ground from its concussion made us unhappy campers, but even that beat the concussion of enemy grenades coming in the night. Yeah, Lai Khe might not have been full of Stateside amenities, but it sure looked good after a mission. At least we had a bunch of 1st Infantry Division troopers with us to provide a little security. Yes, it was home while away from home!

Chapter 26

A Caged Tiger

I awakened suddenly, wondering where I was. Then it came back: the six of us were in double-canopy jungle somewhere around the Angel's Wing, less than a klick from the Cambodian border. A heavy ground fog had rolled in to engulf our tiny defensive perimeter, bringing with it a strange, ominous feeling of doom. Dawn was still a half hour away, and everything was quiet. Too quiet? I looked around slowly to see who was supposed to be on guard duty, only to discover that everybody was sound asleep except me.

What was going on? I asked myself. It was not my watch, so it hadn't been me who had dropped the ball and fallen asleep on guard. Somebody had let the team down, and I was mad. I decided to wake up the entire team. I rolled over and shook the people on both sides of me, but they didn't move. Something was definitely wrong. Slowly, I edged over to the rest of the guys and shook each one, but not one of them responded to my touch.

The eerie fog covered everything, making it impossible to see even my hand. It was almost like a dream, but I knew I wasn't dreaming. Desperate for some kind of answer, I grabbed each of my teammates and shook him violently, but they would still not awaken. Frantic now, I picked up the radio handset to call base for help and discovered that it was dead.

A hint of light was breaking over the horizon, and in its

faint illumination, I could see my surroundings a little better. Crawling around the perimeter to where the TL's position was, I pulled him up to where we were face-to-face. Something warm and sticky ran down my hand. I looked down to discover that it was blood, his blood; his throat had been sliced wide open. It was only then that I realized that everyone on my team was dead except me. Enemy sappers had infiltrated our tight perimeter during the night and had slit everyone's throat—everyone, that is, except me. How had they overlooked me? It had to be the fog! Somehow they had missed me in the fog.

I was shocked by the overwhelming sensation of sheer terror that came over me. Everyone was gone—my entire team dead! I was all alone. What could I do? I fought to get ahold of my emotions, and finally got my wits about me. The terror soon gave way to a sense of outrage stronger than anything I had ever experienced before. Seconds later, I gathered up the radio and my rucksack, grabbed my weapon, and began moving slowly away from the scene of the carnage. A short distance away, I found a dense clump of bushes that would provide temporary shelter and took immediate advantage of it. I needed time to think, to develop a plan of action. And I knew that whatever I did, the radio was my only hope.

In the cover of the thicket, I quickly discovered that the radio's commo cord had been cut, rendering the handset inoperable. As the dawn light slowly crept higher into the sky, I began to realize the magnitude of the predicament I was in. I knew that the enemy would come back when it was light enough for them to assess the damage they had done the night before. They would be looking for maps and code books, and they would take the weapons and any equipment that could be useful to them. I had only two choices—hide, and hit them when they returned, hoping it was a small enough force to destroy alone; escape and evade, and try to make my way back to a friendly base. There were no other alternatives.

I didn't want to leave my teammates behind, but there was no longer anything I could do for them. What was I supposed to do? It was a scenario that none of us had ever trained for or, for that matter, had even thought about. I sat back in the brush, feeling alone and helpless in the middle of a hopeless situation.

It was just beginning to get light when I decided to escape. I took a long drink from my canteen, then moved slowly out of the bushes in the direction of the PZ. If I could get there undetected, choppers would be in the area looking for us. We had missed two of our scheduled sitreps, and the TOC would know something was wrong. There would be a call for an overflight of the team's last reported location, followed by the insertion of a reaction force. If I could hold out without being discovered until the choppers arrived, I had my signal mirror ready to get their attention.

Cautiously, I inched through the jungle, stopping frequently to look and listen. My senses were on full alert as a constant rush of adrenaline kept me pushing onward. The thought that I had left my buddies behind tore at me until the feeling of guilt was almost unbearable, but I knew that if I could get help and get back to them quickly, we could get their bodies out before the enemy got to them. At least they wouldn't be carried as "missing in action." I knew that would help their families deal with the pain.

I moved for nearly an hour, until I stumbled across a high-speed trail running across my route of travel. That stopped me dead. The trail was heading in the same direction as the PZ, so I decided to use it. Oh, I knew that it was never a good idea to run a trail, but in this case, I decided it was worth sacrificing caution for speed.

I began moving faster, determined to find help. Rounding a bend in the trail, I suddenly came face-to-face with two Viet Cong soldiers carrying AK-47s slung over their shoulders. That was their undoing. My M-16 cut both of them down before they had time to react. Quickly, I searched their bodies for any usable intelligence I could find and came up with a map of the area. I stuck it in my cargo pocket, then booby-trapped each of the bodies with a frag before moving on.

The trail began moving away from the PZ, so I crawled

back into the brush to keep on the correct heading. Checking my map and compass frequently allowed me to keep oriented. I figured the PZ couldn't be any more than five hundred meters away.

I shot an azimuth with my compass and began once again to break brush in the direction of the PZ. Eventually, I came to a knoll on the crest of a ridge and stared down on the PZ below. It was only a small clearing in the middle of the jungle, but it was large enough for two or three helicopters. With renewed hope, I began to work my way down into the valley below.

My mouth was dry, and I was out of water. I was sure that a stream lay no more than thirty meters to my front. According to my map, I had to cross it to get to my destination. I crawled carefully to within ten meters of the stream. Looking up and down the banks, I saw no evidence that the enemy was anywhere in the vicinity. I removed an empty canteen from its pouch and moved closer to fill it in the stream.

As the canteen began to take in water, I bent down to take a quick drink from the stream. The water was cool and refreshing, and I closed my eyes to drink deeply to satisfy my thirst. When I opened them again, in the reflection of the water I saw five Viet Cong soldiers standing behind me less than six feet away. Their weapons were pointed at my back.

I was in a bad situation; I had to surrender or die. In a moment of weakness, I decided that I didn't want to die.

They stripped me from the waist up, tied my hands behind my back, then gagged and blindfolded me. I was prodded to get me moving along, and someone behind me shoved me every few steps.

The singsong cadence of the Vietnamese conversing with one another along the march irritated me, and I grew angry as I thought about the lifeless bodies of my teammates lying back there in the jungle. Suddenly, something struck me hard on the back of my head, and the lights went out.

It was impossible to know how long I was out, but I came to, listening to a lot of chatter being carried on in Vietnamese. We were in some kind of village, and there were a lot of Vietnamese civilians gathered around me with sticks. I was in a cage made of bamboo. The civilians started poking me with sharpened bamboo poles, causing the blood to flow freely through my punctured skin. A tremendous thirst came over me, as I suffered in the merciless hot sun. But I knew that no one would come to my aid. A number of women and children showed up later and began taunting me and spitting on me.

After some time elapsed, I passed out again. In my state of painful exhaustion, I dreamed or imagined a bunch of long-haired hippies marching to protest the war. They carried signs that called us "crazy baby killers." Another poster showed Uncle Sam being hanged by the neck. The crowd was burning the American flag.

I awoke in a cold sweat only to discover that it was getting dark. My head was throbbing where someone had belted me. My cage was moving, carried on poles by four Viet Cong. Another VC following close behind saw that I had awakened and jabbed me hard with a sharpened stick. I was being caged and tortured like some wild animal. Where were they taking me? Was this to be my fate—a POW? Would they torture me or just kill me? What would my family be told? Your son is missing in action! (What about my teammates?) What would their families be told? MIA . . . MIA . . . MIA! I began to beat on the cage, screaming in rage, "Let me out of here!"

As in all the times before, I came out of it. I was on my cot in our hootch back at Lai Khe. It was night again, and I had survived another nightmare. As I lay on my back on my sweat-soaked cot, the tears began to well up in my eyes as I thought of the fate of all those young Americans who were missing in action and probably being held by the enemy. I knew that they and their families back home in the States were suffering twenty-four hours a day, every day, yet their lives had to go on.

Sure, my teammates and I were still alive, but what about the next day, or the next week? The biggest problem we had to cope with was the insane rationale behind the war. Were we there to win or not? Why did our leaders refuse to allow us to use the combat tactics that would allow us to prevail over the enemy? Cambodia, Laos, and North Vietnam were safe zones and sanctuaries for the VC and NVA. Why were we not allowed to invade those enemy havens and clean them out? Why weren't we being allowed to take the war to the enemy for a change, to make them fight to defend *their* homelands? If we were there to fight, then why couldn't we go for it all, throw out everything for one big finale, winner take all? Only absolute victory could prevent continued death and destruction. What were the president and Congress waiting for? We only wanted to get the war over with so that we could fly back home and live again like decent human beings.

Imagination and reality clashed, assaulting our minds. What was real and what was not often were hard to factor. The truth was simply that every day was a physical and mental struggle for survival.

Chapter 27

A Recondo Christmas

Project Delta was considered one of the most highly classified Special Forces operations in Vietnam. It was made up of some of the finest and most experienced SF operators in the business.

General Westmoreland had ordered SF to employ the methods they used to train their recon teams and incorporate them into a three-week school that would be located in Nha Trang at the headquarters of the 5th Special Forces Group. The school was named MACV Recondo School and soon became the primary in-country training center for special operations reconnaissance teams, including U.S. LRRPs/LRPs/Rangers, UDT/SEALs, Marine Force and Battalion Recon, air force Air Commandos, and their allied counterparts from South Vietnam, South Korea, Thailand, and Australia. Only soldiers selected by their commanders were awarded precious slots to this school. A high percentage of those attending washed out during the grueling three-week course and were sent back to their units. The course was so good that even those who washed out returned to their units far better trained than before their attendance at the school.

MACV Recondo School was the only military school in existence that required its students to go on an actual combat patrol prior to graduation. Upon completion of the course, successful students were given certificates assigning them a recondo number that was recorded at the Pentagon, and a special patch to wear on their uniforms showing that they were recondo-qualified.

The course was demanding physically, mentally, and emotionally. It combined a good amount of physical training with classroom instruction. This encompassed air, sea, and land infiltration, land navigation—the expert use of compass and map reading—patrolling techniques, medical training, small-team tactics, rappelling, rafting, ambush techniques, radio procedure, and artillery and tac-air coordination.

The cadre teaching the course was a very impressive group of men, some of whom I recognized from my brief tenure with Training Group at Fort Bragg. The men were combat-seasoned senior NCOs who had been serving on A-teams, SOG teams, and with Mobile Strike Force units.

Four of us from 1st Division LRPs attended the course together—Harry Suive, Roberto Rodrigues, Kenneth Whiting, and me. We drew our TDY (temporary duty) pay advances and hopped on a chopper to Di An. There we caught a ride to Saigon, where we spent the night. The next day we boarded another flight to Nha Trang.

What a beautiful city Nha Trang turned out to be. It sat conveniently by the ocean and greeted us with an abundance of sandy, white beaches, pretty girls, French restaurants, and refreshingly pure sea air. The place was a paradise. If and when the war ended, it would make a killer resort.

However, we had no time to enjoy the luxuries of Nha Trang. After checking into Recondo School, everyone was soon busy with studies. We faced three very intense weeks of training, and our focus was directed there.

Each day started very early with a forty-five-minute workout in the sandpit, followed by a daily run. After completing the run, we retired to the mess hall for a full breakfast and then hit the classrooms. Each day's training seemed a little more intense than the preceding day's. During the first week, we focused mainly on physical conditioning, suffering our first casualties and losing many to injuries and sheer exhaustion.

Then there was the seven-and-a-half-mile run at the end of the first week. It wasn't bad enough that we had to run that far in the heat and humidity of Vietnam, but we had to accomplish the task wearing our full combat gear and rappelling equipment. The instructors even added a nice little bonus, a thirty-pound sandbag for each rucksack. With all that added weight, the run still had to be completed in a certain amount of time or we were washed out of the course and sent immediately back to our units. Needless to say, we lost many more students there. Running seven and a half miles in ninety percent humidity, with temperatures in the high nineties to low one hundreds, made the effort difficult enough. Throw in nearly a hundred pounds of gear, and a thirty-pound sandbag bouncing up and down that rubbed the back raw with every step taken. Maybe you can understand why the attrition rate was high.

The run began on a steaming asphalt road, and ended on a sandy beach along the coast. Guard jeeps were stationed all along the course to catch would-be cheaters. I thought that I was in pretty good shape. I always ran a lot and could leg-press over a thousand pounds. But I was in the middle of the pack when my turn came, and believe me I was happy simply to complete the run within the allotted time.

Week two saw far fewer students than were there at the beginning of the course. Many had been terminated or had quit of their own accord. That week, we worked extensively on the rappelling towers and classroom tactics. Oh yeah, we still did the running and the PT; classroom exams and physical fitness tests eliminated still others.

Week three for our class was also Christmas week, 1968. I had made friends with a lot of guys from many different outfits. There were LRPs at the school from nearly every long-range patrol company in Vietnam.

One humorous escapade occurred during our sea infiltration training. We were organized into six-man teams for inflatable raft training. I happened to be in a group with five South Koreans: two Korean Marine NCOs, two ROK Army NCOs, and a ROK Army lieutenant. None of them spoke very good English, but all were superbly seasoned soldiers. I was designated the team leader. We were to paddle out to sea, then turn around and head back to shore. On my command, the team was to capsize the rubber raft with me aboard, then turn it back over again with me still in it.

It was soon our turn. Everything went fine at first. We paddled out into the bay and turned around just as we were supposed to, then I gave the order to capsize the boat. As I held on, they quickly complied, and I soon found myself in the ocean under the raft. They had been instructed to flip the raft over again with me still aboard, but as I waited and waited nothing happened. Finally, when I could no longer hold my breath, I let go of the raft and swam out from under it. When I reached the surface, I found my comrades holding on to the raft and roaring with laughter. I looked across the water at the rest of the group standing on shore and discovered that most of them were laughing, too. Ha-ha, the joke was on me! Everyone had had a good laugh at my expense.

We finally righted the raft, climbed back aboard, and paddled ashore. Some sea infiltration! The enemy would have spotted us a mile from shore. Oh well, laughter always helped to take the edge off a tough training session. Besides, the Koreans seemed to have taken to me, and we were soon friends, although communications remained quite limited.

The remaining students still had one more challenge to face. We had to jump into the water and swim out to an anchored boat, around it, then back to shore again. A Recondo School instructor was on board to make sure we didn't touch or grab the boat. Exhausted and somewhat waterlogged, I somehow completed the swim and made it back to shore alive. However, once again, we lost more of our classmates.

Christmas day arrived, a sad day for us; our thoughts went back to family and home. That evening, several of us sat around a table in the club drinking, playing slot machines, and just talking. I shared a table with my five South Korean teammates. Most of the conversation was in Korean, so I did a lot more listening than talking. I paid more attention to the jukebox and kept it operating. The South Koreans kept slapping me on the back to assure me that I was their friend, but the gesture didn't help. I was still the outsider at the table. So much for my social life!

Back at the barracks that evening, sirens signaled a red alert, waking everyone. We were told that an enemy ground probe was possibly in the making, and we were quickly assigned as perimeter guards. However, after a few hours of waiting, nothing materialized—there was no assault, no probe, no sappers, or anything else of a hostile nature. But we did get to watch one awesomely incredible pyrotechnic display out on the slopes of Grand Summit Mountain.

A Special Forces team was in contact, and tracers were flying everywhere. The mountain was erupting in the midst of a serious firefight. Flares and red and green tracers lit up the night sky. An intense battle was taking place. Men were fighting and dying while we watched silently and safely from the perimeter.

Suddenly, the sky opened up and disgorged deadly ribbons of death and destruction on the NVA forces in the jungle below. Puff the Magic Dragon had arrived on the scene to support the surrounded team with its awesome firepower. Crimson streamers arced out into the night and pounded the enemy positions as the C-47 gunship orbited high overhead with its miniguns blazing. Merry Christmas, 1968!

Finally, the day of our graduation mission was at hand. Seven of us boarded a chopper and headed out to Grand Summit Mountain. Six of us were Recondo students; the seventh team member was an SF Recondo School cadre.

I took point after the chopper dropped us off on a ridge and flew off into the sunset. I moved the team into a nearby bamboo thicket as darkness closed in around us. We were positioned about halfway up the mountain in very heavy cover and decided that it was a good place to RON. By then, darkness had overtaken us. There was no moon, and the night was simply black. We set up one-man guard shifts forty-five minutes long, and the rest of us tried to grab a little sleep.

Shortly after midnight, just as I began my watch, I heard

the muffled sounds of someone talking in Vietnamese somewhere below us. It was far enough away that I didn't see the need to awaken the rest of the team.

The distant conversation went on for quite a while, finally becoming very quiet near the end of my shift. I was fighting off sleepiness, when a sudden crashing sound up on the ridge above us brought me to full alert. It sounded like someone or something large had fallen heavily in the jungle just above our position.

Then an eerie sound began that sent chills up my spine, and I turned to make sure that the team was awake. Believe me, the noise soon commanded everyone's fullest attention. The sound of intense, heavy breathing echoed down toward us. It had to be some kind of animal. And whatever it was, it was coming closer. It stopped about forty to fifty meters from us, but the heavy panting and gasping continued for quite a while. We could forget sleeping. At that moment, everyone on the team was wide awake and on a 101 percent alert.

Just before first light, we gathered up our gear, sterilized our RON, and prepared to move out. Only a short distance from where we had spent the night, we discovered the unmistakable pug marks of a large tiger. They were *massive* prints. I could put both of my hands inside a single paw mark. We had heard of guys being attacked and eaten by tigers in Vietnam, but we always figured those were just "war stories." That turned out to be the most exciting part of the mission.

When it came time to pull in our horns and get out of the area, our extraction went off smoothly, and we were soon back in Nha Trang.

We graduated from Recondo School a short time later. I was given a Recondo certificate showing that I had graduated in class R-13-69. We were soon on our way back to our units, a lot better trained and more highly motivated than we were before. We had gained a lot of self-confidence and had mastered some valuable tricks and techniques during our three weeks at Recondo School that we would soon be employing against the enemy. Those three weeks leading up to Christmas, 1968, will forever be etched on my mind. It wasn't exactly the Merry Christmas one would dream of having, but we had survived and faced a new year.

In addition to Harry Suive, Kenneth Whiting, and me from the 1st Infantry Division LRPs, our graduating class included men from 5th SF Group, U.S. Navy SEALs, U.S. Air Force Air Commandos, 1st Cav Division, 4th Infantry Division, 9th Infantry Division, 25th Infantry Division, 5th Mech Division, 199th Light Infantry Brigade, 82d Airborne Division, 173d Airborne Brigade, 101st Airborne Division, and ROK Marine Division.

I had also met Sgt. Lawrence D. Closson from Company F, 58th Infantry (LRP), 101st Airborne, who would later endure many harrowing missions with that unit. All of us had stories in the making.

Back in Lai Khe, Suive, Whiting, and I hooked back up with our teammates and the war.

Chapter 28

Nightmare Eve, 1968

The final day of 1968 was a very somber one for the LRPs of the Big Red One. It was to prove very costly for us.

Intelligence got the word that the enemy was planning to hit Lai Khe with a major rocket attack in the near future. Somebody came up with the brilliant idea of sending out the LRPs in platoon force to stop them. While I was still away at Recondo School, thirty of our men were to walk out of the perimeter and do their best to prevent rocket attacks on Lai Khe. Since the range of an NVA 122mm rocket was somewhere around eight to nine miles, the likelihood of thirty LRPs successfully patrolling the entire area inside the eight-to-nine-mile diameter of the target was next to nil. But the voice of reason was often absent at division staff; the mission was a "go."

Lieutenant Davis, First Sergeant Cook, and newly promoted Sergeant First Class Mattoon were to lead the operation. They decided that the most efficient way to use our group was as a force multiplier. They would allow us to break up into six-man teams to patrol during the day, and then come back together as a platoon each night for safety in numbers. One must admit that the plan made a lot of sense, given the fact that we couldn't get the mission scrubbed. We were more effective working in six-man teams. We could also cover more ground much faster if we broke up into smaller components rather than staying together. And thirty men would have a much easier time defending themselves if attacked in a night perimeter than six would.

When the platoon walked out of the perimeter, they noticed a large number of civilians working the fields outside the base, and they were looking our group over closely as they moved past them. That was not common behavior for the local farmers, who usually ignored Americans completely when we were on patrol. All the attention made everyone uneasy.

When the platoon reached the jungle, our point man immediately located a prominent trail junction. Mattoon suggested that it was a good time to divide up into four teams to check out the trails in all four directions. Davis and Cook agreed with the plan, but before anyone had a chance to implement it, an explosion occurred toward the rear of the patrol. John Douglas and a relatively new LRP tripped a booby trap on the trail behind the unit and were wounded. It was serious enough that both men had to be medevacked out.

After the wounded were taken care of, everyone broke into teams and moved off to check out the four trails. Ron Crews moved his team down one of the trails with Reynaldo Arenas at point. After progressing only a short distance, another loud explosion occurred.

The other three teams quickly moved back to the trail junction and linked up again; Crew's team failed to show up. Setting up a defensive perimeter around the trail junction, Lieutenant Davis sent one man down the trail Crews had taken. He reported back ten minutes later that Crews's team was down with one KIA and one WIA. As the rest of the platoon moved cautiously but quickly down the trail to render aid, another Dustoff helicopter was summoned to evacuate the casualties.

When our force reached Crews's team, it was discovered that Ron Crews was severely wounded and Reynaldo Arenas was dead. They had apparently walked up on a command-detonated mine, and the enemy had blown it in their faces. The Lurps had a difficult time putting Arenas's body and the badly wounded Crews aboard the medevac and then continuing the mission.

There were still twenty-six angry Lurps left as they moved in one group down the main trail leading away from the junction. It wasn't long before the men began finding booby traps all around them. Most of them were simple grenade traps rigged with trip wires. Everyone pulled back to call in a fire mission to soften up the area and detonate the booby traps. On the way back, they spotted more booby traps just off the trail. Charlie had made his plans well, just in case we had decided to parallel the trails as we normally did.

As artillery began to pound the area, there were a number of secondary explosions, a few of them much too large for grenades. The Lurps hoped that the artillery had managed to hit some of the enemy's rockets.

After the force had finished the patrol and moved back toward the perimeter, it was discovered that the civilians were no longer working in the rice paddies. This suggested that, at the very least, they had managed to contact their neighborhood Victor Charles and notify him of our numbers and direction, which would explain the large number of booby traps strewn along our path and our subsequent casualties.

Crews was gravely wounded, and we did not know if he would survive. Douglas and the new man were also wounded, but not as badly as Crews. And Arenas was dead. The casualties left the entire company shocked and in mourning.

Why had that happened to us? Why were we being used as infantrymen? We searched among ourselves for answers and came up empty-handed. Our ranks continued to thin, and that kind of misuse just didn't make any sense. Good men kept dying and were being maimed for life on humbug missions sent down from above. Someone needed to wake up before it was too late. At times like that, we felt helpless.

New Year's Day was the cause of much grief back at the LRP compound that year. There was no celebration, no parties, no welcoming in the New Year for us. We had lost four of our brothers. Crews, Douglas, and the new man had been evacuated back to the World, and Arenas paid the ultimate price for someone's stupidity. He was a great person, and we missed him as a friend and a valuable, experienced long-range patroller.

I had been a LRP for three months, and my attitude about Vietnam had changed since I had first arrived in country. My original desire, to stop communism in its tracks, was beginning to look impossible. We could not win the war with our hands tied behind our backs. We could only take more senseless casualties. Since General Westmoreland helped initiate Lurps and defined what our role would be, why were we being used contrary to our job description? Our size and training dictated that we be either operating on long-range patrols (which might involve combat) or long-range reconnaissance patrols. That is, our duties included pure recon, ambush, prisoner snatch, POW rescue, and rescuing downed aircraft crews. If we continued being misused on short-range ventures, additional disaster would sooner or later come knocking.

Chapter 29

Melancholy Moments

Hello Folks,

How do I describe the feelings we have been enduring over here? This place resembles the outer limits of the world. One day springs forth in base camp with some semblance of civilization; the next day we're out in the jungle living like animals.

One day finds us trying to rest and relax and stand down from the adrenaline rush of combat; tomorrow, we'll be back out fighting for our lives.

Today, we look at children and women here at the base. They are victims of the war hoping only to survive it. It is our job to protect them. Tomorrow we will be out looking for some more of their countrymen to kill before they try to kill us.

Today, we listen to music on a radio or record player that reminds us of home. Tomorrow we will listen to the sorrowful sound of "Taps" being played at a memorial service for another fallen brother.

Today, we read two-week-old copies of Stateside newspapers, telling us what's happening back home. Hippies are having love-ins while smoking dope and calling us inhumane. College students are marching in protest of the war and giving comfort and encouragement to our enemies.

Some movie star is posing for a photo straddling an NVA antiaircraft gun somewhere on the outskirts of Hanoi.

Tomorrow, we read the obituary column in the current issue of *Stars & Stripes* to see if we recognize any of the names of the KIAs.

However, the letters you send let us know that we are still loved and missed. The goodies that you bake us are inhaled by the entire team. Food from home sure tastes great, even if it's a little stale. Kool-Aid makes the water taste bearable, too. Say, what is the latest fashion craze back there? Cammo is still the rage over here.

At times, it is so lonely here; the days barely seem to creep by. Yet, at other times, the stress of the situation is so intense. Our emotions seem to be riding a giant roller coaster. This is certainly a horrible place to rot. But of course, rotting takes time. Some are quickly taken due to accidents, bullets, or shrapnel.

Funny, I remember how bored I was sitting in class back at college. Nothing seemed interesting to me except some distant land called Vietnam. Now, I would love to be back home attending class or working somewhere. Yes, and driving my '62 Corvette would sure feel good. I can almost picture myself behind the wheel with a beautiful girl riding shotgun. And I really miss coaching peewee football and boys baseball.

Fishing up at Lake Bridgeport would be awesome right now. Hauling in those big crappie sure sounds wonderful. And what I would give to be around a campfire talking about tomorrow morning's deer hunt. How neat a really boring life would be right now if I were at home with my family and friends. This place seems like another planet.

Chief Vaughn Isaacs, and I just returned from the Beer Garden here at Lai Khe. We enjoyed their homemade French fries. Also, the female Vietnamese barber was pretty. She gives a good haircut and massage while one sits in the barber chair.

Well, they're getting up a football game out beside one of our hootches. I guess that I'll go get in on it. Life goes on here in sunny, exotic Southeast Asia, but how I want to go home! I suppose this letter is about to conclude for now. Please write me when you can.

Serving,
Bill

P.S. One day I look forward to getting on that freedom bird and flying across the big pond back into your lives and real freedom.

Chapter 30

The Hot Spot

Not long after New Year's Day, 1969, I went out on a mission as part of a heavy team. It was uncommon for us to operate in ten-man teams, so this was a new experience for a lot of us.

Lt. Jerry Davis, our company commander, went with us. He was the only officer in the unit that we really respected. I guess that he had earned our respect because he was the only one who had the guts to go out on patrols with us and share the danger and the suffering we were exposed to. He truly cared about us, and he even broke the officers' code by associating with his enlisted personnel outside his official capacity as our commanding officer. Jerry Davis was Ranger-qualified (meaning he'd graduated Ranger school in the United States, an extremely difficult course), and he knew how to be a leader and a teammate at the same time. He led us by example, and he led us well. I can pay him no greater tribute than that.

After our insertion, we moved immediately into a dense stand of woods where we found much sign of heavy enemy use. There were a number of well-used trails leading in and out of the trees. On the other side of the tree line lay an expansive rice paddy. It was a good place to set up an ambush, so we placed our M-60 covering a bend in one of the main trails that snaked directly into our kill zone.

Out to our front sprawled an open area, maybe seventy meters across. On the other side of it ran a stream, where the dinks had cut a large tree so that it had fallen across the river to serve as a footbridge. There was also a small secondary trail leading into the ambush site from a different direction. We were in a very precarious position, so "alert" was the password for the mission.

Lieutenant Davis and I lay side by side, monitoring the footbridge. Other team members watched the remaining avenues of approach. Nothing out of the ordinary occurred for quite some time, then things began to pop.

First, a group of five VC moved up along the far side of the stream toward the footbridge. But they stopped just short of it, and one of them, wearing a pair of binoculars around his neck, climbed a tall tree. When he reached the upper branches, he used the binoculars to check out the area. First, he scanned out across the large rice paddy behind us, then he started working his way back closer to the stream, including the area where we lay in ambush. When he was looking directly at us, he suddenly jerked the binoculars away and pretended to be intent on observing a different area. Lieutenant Davis and I fired pretty much simultaneously, knocking the VC out of the tree and into the stream.

Everyone began firing on the remaining four VC as they broke and tried to run away. After they disappeared around the bend in the trail, some of us were sent over to check out the kill zone. We recovered a couple of RPG grenade launchers and the tire-sole sandals from the VC we had shot out of the tree. We moved quickly back to our side of the stream and resumed our positions. We would wait for a while to see if anyone else decided to show up to find out what all the shooting had been about.

Suddenly, several VC came storming around a bend in one of the other trails entering our position. Unfortunately, they found themselves staring straight down the muzzle of our M-60 from a distance of less than twenty meters. Expecting to hear the sweet chattering of the M-60, we were stupefied when we heard the sound of a single *click*. The machine gun would not fire! Reacting as one, we began popping them with M-16s and CAR-15s.

Things started to escalate as the enemy returned fire. Over the next few minutes, it got so intense that we had to call in artillery. When the 105mm rounds began impacting among the enemy positions, the VC moved in closer to our positions to avoid the deadly shells. They were not stupid. They knew that we could bring in the artillery only so close without endangering ourselves. So, already low on ammo and in dire straits ourselves, we did the last thing the enemy expected— we called in the artillery almost directly on top of our positions.

That was a first time for me. My pucker factor went off the charts as I tried to burrow into the ground beneath me. We could hear the shrapnel whirring through the air two or three feet over our heads. Pieces of tree and debris began to fall all around us. It was terrifying. I could only imagine what it had to be for the enemy. The sounds of the artillery rounds impacting so close sent chills through us, but it did the trick of breaking up the enemy assault on our positions.

When it was finally over, the VC were gone, and there was devastation everywhere around us. I gained a very healthy respect and sense of appreciation for our artillery that day. Properly directed, it could be very accurate and extremely potent.

After we made sure that the VC were truly gone, we made our way to the PZ and were extracted without a hitch. The patrol could have been better, but it also could have been worse. We had dealt the enemy some damage and misery without having taken any casualties of our own. To us it was a good mission; any mission was good if we returned without casualties.

Chapter 31

Ambush Bay

In January 1969, an unusual mission was posted for one of our teams. The patrol was to be sent down south to work out of the area around the Tu Duc water plant. The insertion was to be by U.S. Navy PBR ("patrol boat, river") boat. Usually, our teams were inserted by helicopter, but the terrain around the Tu Duc water plant was dominated by swamps, mud, muck, and thick brush.

Sgt. Julian Rincon's team got the mission. Made up of Crawley, Wiggins, Busby, and a new man, the team was one of the more experienced teams in the company. They climbed aboard the PBR manned by the sailors of the "brown water" navy, and headed south out into the main river channel. Not far from their AO they quickly turned and moved rapidly up a nearby tributary. Arriving quietly at their drop-off point, the LRPs jumped off the front of the PBR and disappeared into the dense jungle paralleling the shore. They didn't stop until they reached their observation point along the water's edge.

Meanwhile, the boat continued motoring upstream for another mile or so where it would slip quietly into a cove to hide. All was soon quiet except for the monotonous droning of thousands of hungry mosquitoes.

A few hours later, the LRPs detected movement downstream from their position. The team leader contacted the PBR boat by radio and alerted it to be ready for the impending action. Soon, the team observed four motorized sampans coming down the river in the darkness.

As the enemy floated by the LRRP's position, the team leader gave the word to the gunboat. The PBR cranked up and charged downstream at full throttle. Just before it reached the VC sampans, it unleashed a massive barrage of .50-caliber and small-arms fire. Riddled, two of the sampans sank in midstream. The other two managed to escape before the patrol boat could close up. Three or four enemy soldiers died in the action while the friendlies sustained no casualties. Chalk up a successful joint ambush! The PBR circled a couple of times, then pulled into shore to pick up the waiting long-range patrol, then backed out into midstream and sped away from Ambush Bay.

With all of the high-tech weapons we had at our disposal, we could have won the war convincingly and in a very short period of time. Why we were not allowed to finish it once and for all and go home was beyond common sense. We should have been allowed to go on the offensive and take the ground war to North Vietnam. With us taking the initiative, Hanoi would have been forced to fight the ground war on its own turf. Instead, all it had to do was to avoid periodic bombing and repair what little damage we managed to inflict. It was the wrong way to defeat a determined and committed enemy.

What could our leaders have possibly been thinking? Good men were dying every day, but we were not gaining any ground or achieving any measure of success. We won all the major fights and drove the enemy from every battlefield, only to withdraw when the battle was over and allow the enemy to move back in. Then we would start over again, repeating the same mad scenario. If we were going to fight, bleed, and die, then the deaths should count for something important, like liberating the oppressed or stopping tyranny and aggression. We had always been taught that when you played the game, you played to win. Why didn't it apply in this situation? Maybe no one taught our politicians how to play to win, and this was not a game!

Chapter 32

Zoology 101 R.V.N.

One of the many things we had to become accustomed to involved the variety of animal life in Vietnam. Some of the animals there were also indigenous to the United States, some were not. In base camp, we had many familiar sights such as dogs, chickens, rats, birds, monkeys, snakes, ants, mosquitoes, bugs, worms, butterflies, and such.

However, in the jungle, we might also see hostile water buffalo, elephants, tigers, leopards, panthers, lizards, giant earthworms, leeches, varieties of monkeys, mongooses, and some species we couldn't even identify. The jungle appeared to accommodate many hidden secrets, always making one speculate on his next encounter.

Daytime in the boonies was always scorching and stifling, so we were always soaking wet. Snakes were quite active in that climate, and Nam had many varieties of venomous snakes. Scorpions were numerous and certain varieties were very poisonous in Southeast Asia. And even the areas with beautiful beaches had deadly sea snakes swimming along with sharks.

Probably the most bothersome of all of the creatures to deal with were the hordes of roaming, giant, blood-sucking mosquitoes, relentless enemies that attacked day and night in the hootch or in the jungle, in rice paddies or on the beach. At least they were not too choosy when lunchtime came. Mosquitoes feasted on male and female, soldier, sailor, air force, Marine, coast guard, and civilian, enjoying the blood of communist and capitalist. Protestant, Catholic, Jew, and everyone else became featured entrées on the mosquito's menu. They enjoyed white, brown, yellow, or black skin. The little nasties were the ultimate guerrilla warriors, striking anywhere and anytime as masters of the ambush. Yes, they were also airborne dive bombers. The only safe haven from their assault was under water, and we could not manage to hold our breaths very long down under.

We could not fight back against them very well. When one was squashed, the blood attracted more. Mosquito repellent helped a little, but it did not last. It slowed them for a short time, but it never stopped them. Yes, they were our most successful enemy. And some of the air pirates carried vivax or falciparum malaria, a bonus for their unfortunate victims.

Some nights in the bush were almost unbearable. With everything else we had to be concerned about, we still had the relentless mosquitoes to deal with. They got all over our faces, ears, eyes, noses, mouths, throats, and other parts, injecting their stingers and extracting our blood. Also, their constant buzzing could almost drive a person crazy.

Another pest we often encountered was the leech, the small crawling vampires. They attacked us from land and water. Crossing streams usually meant we likely had parasitical passengers by the time we got to the bank. Sometimes we had to inspect one another to rid ourselves of the freeloaders. On land, they raised up and searched us out, then they managed to crawl up inside our clothes and attach themselves to our bodies. After that, the creatures extracted our blood into themselves until they were so swollen that they sometimes exploded. Often they left awful marks on us, a sign of dining on our iron-rich blood. We doused leeches with mosquito repellent and popped them when they let loose of their hold.

Then there were the ants. Fire ants and giant red jungle ants were very carnivorous. They could be found on bushes, trees, or the ground, and they attacked us with a vengeance. Hundreds of them would climb on one of us in a matter of seconds, all vying for a meal. The stings felt like fire igniting all over the body. Huge ugly welts or blisters were trademarks of their attacks.

The gnats were really annoying, too. They seemed to enjoy flying in our ears and mouths; they buzzed around and landed on us all night long, and their constant racket really played on our nerves. They were most definitely pests, though they did not inflict wounds.

But the major carnivores, the leopards, panthers, and tigers were always in the back of our minds. Because of them, we certainly slept lightly out in the bush. We didn't relish the mighty purr of the big cats.

Of course, we always had the ever-present snakes to watch out for. When lying on the ground at night, that was a major concern. Cobras, bamboo vipers, and a host of others could definitely put the hurt on their victims. Not all snakes in Vietnam were poisonous; some of them could squeeze their prey and swallow it whole. The wildlife of Vietnam provided a lot of intrigue for our imaginations.

If a person did not get shot, bit, or stung while spending his tour in country, he simply was not really there! It was a hostile environment even without the Viet Cong and NVA messing with us, but they were willing to make us unwelcome as well. Vietnam was not only a 365-day tour of duty; it was an everyday education. We all took Zoology 101, Republic of Vietnam style. We discovered that class could be in session in even the most exotic—and beautiful—settings. And one had better learn quickly; a failing grade could lead to the only early out no one in Vietnam wanted.

Chapter 33

Changing Colors

February 1, 1969, ushered in a major change for all LRPs and LRRPs in Vietnam. The Department of the Army decided to revive the old Ranger heritage. Thereafter, all long-range patrol units became lettered companies of the 75th Infantry (Ranger). We would still be attached to the same parent divisions, field forces, and brigades, as before, but we would all be united under a single banner.

Our unit was deactivated from Company F, 52d Infantry (LRP), then reactivated as Company I, 75th Infantry (Ranger). Each new Ranger company was assigned a letter of the alphabet. The Americal Division LRPs became Company G, 75th Infantry (Ranger); the 1st Cavalry Division LRPs became Company H, 75th Infantry (Ranger); the 101st Airborne Division LRPs became Company L, 75th Infantry (Ranger). And so on.

Every infantry division still retained special long-range patrolling capabilities with their attached Ranger companies. The 1st Infantry Division continued to be blessed with us, but we were to be called Rangers instead of LRPs. The change would take a little getting used to, but it was probably a good thing. However, our ranks were still pretty thin; we continued to lose personnel through wounds, death, and rotation home.

On the lighter side, an event occurred that provided us all with a little entertainment. For quite a while, we had been enjoying the antics of a pet monkey someone had brought into the company area. The little spider monkey liked to sit on people's heads and search their hair for fleas, lice, and other tasty tidbits.

Well, one day the little monkey urinated on someone's head. No one knew why he did it, but the fact remained that he had tinkled on a LRP's head, and *no one* emptied its bladder on a LRP. The next thing we knew, the monkey was simply no longer around. No one knew what had happened to him; he just wasn't there anymore. We suspected foul play, but no one could prove anything. We suspected that he was the victim of a little monkey business.

Things really began to heat up for us after our unit was re-designated. We began to get more missions at the same time we were getting a lot of new replacements into the company and they needed a lot of training. We had to cannibalize downtime teams just to get full teams together for mission assignments, which meant that the seasoned Rangers were getting a lot less time between missions, and there were fewer people in the company area qualified to train the new men.

Typically, we were given three days between a warning order and an upcoming mission, but in early 1969, that was cut to one or two days. At times, we were given only a two-day turnaround between missions, which was not enough time to get ourselves physically and mentally prepared for another launch, especially for those of us who were walking point on the patrols. Giving up downtime was a price that few of us could afford to pay.

One day, I received a big surprise. Lieutenant Davis walked over and handed me a piece of paper. He told me that he knew that things had been rough lately and that I needed to take some time off to get a little rest. I didn't know what he was talking about until I looked down at the paper and saw that it was a seven-day leave to Japan. I couldn't have been happier if he had told me the war was over. Seven whole days without a care or a worry would be wonderful! I could hardly wait to get packed. The mysteries of the Land of the Rising Sun awaited me, and I intended to experience them ASAP.

But it became very difficult to make the transition in my mind from the battlefield to recreation even though I was certainly giving it an effort. So I packed my few belongings and took a chopper ride to Saigon. There I caught a freedom bird (commercial airliner) outbound.

Chapter 34

The Rising Sun

Japan has long been known to the Western world as the Land of the Rising Sun. Stories abound about its charm and inherent beauty. Now I was being given the opportunity to experience that beauty for myself. The relatively short flight was the first true comfort I had experienced since arriving in Vietnam. The temperature aboard the commercial aircraft was comfortable, and the stewardesses and the food were quite nice. It didn't take long before I was able to move the heat, humidity, and stress of Vietnam to the back of my mind.

After landing near Tokyo, the aircraft taxied toward the arrival area. All of us were wearing summer-issue khakis, and we were totally unprepared for the shock that hit us when we deplaned; it was the middle of winter in Japan, and the temperature was in the teens. Snow covered everything. Suddenly, we were acting like kids, diving headfirst into the snow and throwing snowballs at one another. Of course, that didn't last too long because we began to freeze. We barely survived the sprint to the terminal building.

Inside the modern, heated terminal, we were ushered to a reception area run by the U.S. military, where we were given a short briefing on the "do's" and "don'ts" for our weeklong stay in Japan. Then we were given our necessary papers and allowed time to purchase winter clothing.

Seeing Mount Fuji close up and riding the bullet train

were two of the things I really wanted to experience in Japan. Several of us made our way to the train station to catch a ride on the bullet train, which was capable of speeds of nearly two hundred miles per hour. As we climbed aboard, I made my way straight to the dining car to consume my first full meal outside since arriving in Vietnam. The menu looked quite interesting, and I finally decided to order curried chicken. It was absolutely wonderful. After several months of dehydrated LRRP rations and canned C rations, the meal was simply exquisite.

The best part of dining aboard the train was being able to observe the countryside as we sped through it. The only problem was that at two hundred miles per hour, everything closer than a mile was only a blur. But I could see that Japan was indeed a beautiful country, and I was even more impressed when we finally arrived at the town of Atomi, at the base of Mount Fuji. I caught a ride to Hotel New Fugia, a very fancy establishment that offered first-class rooms and first-class service. I was impressed.

I spent the first day touring the town and meeting other U.S. servicemen on R & R from Vietnam. We ate, drank, and observed the many sights of Atomi. Then we took the bus tour up Mount Fujiyama to eight thousand feet, where we stopped to view a beautiful palace that was owned by a prince. It had been built on the shoreline of a gorgeous mountain lake from which fountains shot water high into the air. Looking down from that altitude, we could see the Pacific Ocean filtered through a layer of thin cloud cover. It reminded me of one of the beautiful oil paintings I occasionally saw in Oriental restaurants back in the States. When I saw one of those paintings, I used to think, If any place could really be that pretty, I would sure love to be there. Well, I certainly got my wish!

The road up the mountain ended at the palace. To go on to the summit required that we ride in cable cars. When we got to the top, I was even more amazed at the view. What a place! We were informed that the summit reached nearly fourteen thousand feet above sea level.

At the top we found that some inspired soul had erected an indoor ice-skating rink, which several of the guys wanted to try. I told them that I didn't know how to ice-skate, but I was a pretty fair roller skater. They finally talked me into making an attempt, and skating was really great. With a little practice I could glide around with ease. It was very similar to roller skating in a lot of ways. However, stopping remained a different story altogether. All I could do to brake to a halt was to slam into a wall. It got the job done. At least the ice skating got our minds off the war for a while.

Back in Atomi, we attended a sukiyaki party, which proved to be a real gas. Chopsticks and I did not get along!

But time seemed to fly by, and before I knew it, my leave was drawing to an end. I checked out of Hotel New Fugia and caught a ride back to the terminal to meet the bullet train for the return trip. During the journey, I allowed myself to think about home, family, friends, and life in general. I couldn't help but wonder about what awaited me back in country at Lai Khe. What had happened in my absence? Was everyone okay? I couldn't help but worry. Those guys were a part of me, my brothers in arms. They were more than just friends and comrades. They had become my family. It is very difficult to explain to the uninitiated the type of bond we formed. Once a LRP/Ranger, one was always a LRP/Ranger. I would come to realize that the sense of perpetual bonding was always right there where I could see it, feel it, and live it.

I slept on the plane most of the way back to Vietnam, a journey that seemed quicker than the flight to Japan. When we landed at Tan Son Nhut, I once again was met by the blast furnace welcome of heat and humidity that Vietnam was famous for. The Land of the Rising Sun would always hold many fond memories for me, but I was back in my real world, one of bombs, bullets, booby traps, and bloodshed.

Chapter 35

A Giant Good-bye

We arrived in Saigon and processed back in to the military system. When I was finished, I caught a flight out to Di An, a huge 1st Infantry Division base camp. From there, it was no problem hitching a ride on a Huey flying out to Lai Khe along Highway 13, better known as Thunder Road, because of all the ambushes and mines along its treacherous length.

Once back at our company area, I headed directly for the team hootch. No one was there, so I reported in to the TOC. That was when I found out that two of our teams had been hit hard while I was gone, and I was shocked to discover that one of the teams had been my own. Two of my teammates had been wounded and had been medevacked to our MASH hospital in Lai Khe. I left the company without permission and went in search of the MASH unit. I found the hospital and soon located my two wounded comrades. Don "Giant" Hildebrandt, my team leader, and Bob Lowry were the ones who'd gotten hit. I was able to visit them for a short time, but long enough to find out what had happened and to discover that they were about to be shipped out of country. It looked like they would both recover well in time, but for them, the war was over.

The two Rangers told me that they had gone out the 19th of February. Hildebrandt was the team leader and point man on the mission, and Lowry was walking his slack. Freddie

Blankenship was the RTO. Tony Markovitch served as the ATL and carried the M-79 grenade launcher. Rodney Hayashi brought up the team's rear. We had been working in six-man teams, but while I was on leave in Japan, Hildebrandt decided to walk point himself and go out with five men instead of six rather than take somebody along the team knew nothing about.

The team launched out of Thunder Two, a firebase between Lai Khe and Di An, and moved out into the always uninviting Song Be Corridor. The insertion seemed to go undetected, so the team decided to release the air support and Charlie Mike. Nothing unusual occurred the first day. During the evening, they set up an ambush along a high-speed trail and waited, but no one came calling.

As daylight approached, the five Rangers continued the patrol. Giant moved out on point, and the rest of the team took their positions behind him. It was soon full daylight, and the heat was already beginning to intensify. Giant came upon a well-used high-speed trail. As he looked to the left, he spotted two NVA standing about thirty meters away with maybe seven or eight more farther down the trail.

Giant had been stepping out on the trail when he first saw the NVA. There was nothing for him to do but open up on full automatic. He succeeded in knocking down the first two, but the rest of the NVA scattered. When Giant turned to jump back into the jungle, he took three rounds in his left leg before he could reach cover. A firefight broke out between the two forces, and Lowry caught a round in his left forearm.

The enemy broke contact after a brief but vicious exchange of fire. The team took advantage of the break in the action to evade to a nearby bomb crater, and they called for gunships, an extraction slick, and a medevac. After patching up their wounded teammates, the LRPs sat back to wait for extraction. Soon they heard the unmistakable sounds of the gunships approaching. The team marked its position, and the gunships began firing up the area around them.

The medevac picked up Lowry and Hildebrandt, and then the slick moved in to pick up the rest of the team. Giant and

Lowry were flown to the MASH unit and admitted, while the
rest of the team was flown back to Lai Khe.

It was painful for me to have to leave my wounded comrades, but the war continued without them. I bid them good-
bye and wished them speedy recoveries. I did not see them
again because they were flown out of country immediately
after I left. Their departure left another void for me. Transition seemed to be a constant happening, and normality had
no place with us.

Back at the Ranger compound, I was informed about the
other team that had been hit. One of my closest friends, Bob
Law, was killed on the mission. I was stunned. Bob and I
went back farther than the LRPs. Blood, guts, death, despair,
and duty had now become my constant companions.

Chapter 36

Law's Legacy

Sp4. Bob Law was one of those guys you just liked to hang around. He called the Fort Worth, Texas, area home, just as I did, but we first got acquainted at Fort Polk, Louisiana, where Bob and I were in the same company and same platoon during basic training.

Bob was one of those quiet, unassuming, caring people. He was a little older than most of us and a lot more mature.

After basic, we went in different directions, never expecting to see each other again. I was shocked but pleasantly surprised when I arrived in Lai Khe several months later and discovered that Bob was already there in the LRPs.

While I was attending Special Forces training group, Bob was in country LRPing the boonies. We had a great visit, and he gave me some good advice about our outfit. However, we only managed to go out together on a few missions as we were normally on different teams.

Bob carried a nickname that had been given to him by some of the guys in the company. They called him "Outlaw." It wasn't because of any rebellious attitude that he had been given the name, but because of his lean, rugged, rawboned build, and the long handlebar mustache he wore. All the guys in the company liked Bob. I don't think he had an enemy anywhere.

Bob was a real asset to his team. He could work any position on a mission, and do it well. If you needed him to walk rear security, you knew you'd have a dependable man watching the team's backside. Point, slack, grenadier, or RTO position—it didn't make any difference. Bob simply fit in anywhere he was needed.

While I was on leave, his team was deployed into the area around the Song Be, always a nasty place to patrol. Raymond Cervantes was the team leader on the mission. Michael Cannon walked point, Daniel Wiggins served as the assistant team leader and walked rear security, and Bill Powell humped the PRC-25. Robert Roossien carried the M-79 grenade launcher on the patrol, and Bob Law was in the number-two, slack spot, a position he was very good at.

That was a very solid team, and each of those men was a personal friend of mine. Roossien and I arrived in country almost at the same time. Powell was another migrant from Special Forces and also hailed from Texas.

About an hour after their insertion, Cannon, while walking point, heard someone coughing close by. At the same time, Wiggins detected movement behind them and observed an enemy soldier. Cervantes signaled the team to move to their PZ, since he felt they were almost certainly compromised.

A short time later, the team reached the soggy PZ on a little tributary of the Song Be. They set up in a wagon-wheel defensive perimeter and waited for the extraction ship and escort to arrive.

Outlaw soon spotted some VC that seemed to be following the team. A brief firefight broke out just as the gunships arrived on station. The Cobras made several runs on the VC positions firing rockets and miniguns, but the team was forced to move, and the men jumped into a stream as Powell called for an immediate extraction. His request was denied because it was almost dark. Because the team had suffered no injuries or deaths, and was no longer in contact, the decision was made to leave them in overnight. Obviously, someone in a position to make decisions was not considering the well-being of a small six-man team!

Later that night, the team slipped down the stream and

across a shallow swamp. They spotted a small footbridge that crossed the Suoi Ong Bang tributary of the Song Be. After calling in a sitrep to base, they received orders to remain there and observe the bridge. Gathering into a tight defensive position, the team monitored the bridge for the rest of the evening and all the next day and night.

Around 0800 hours on the morning of February 22, the situation went sour, then escalated, as three VC carrying AK-47s and one RPD machine gun approached the bridge. Apparently, the VC spotted the Rangers hiding nearby, and commenced firing. All three of the enemy soldiers were quickly wounded, but they continued to fight and tossed grenades at the Ranger team.

Powell radioed in the contact. He requested artillery and gunships, since he suspected that more enemy soldiers were likely to appear on the scene at any moment. The Rangers had remained in the same spot much too long, but they had been following orders.

Bob Law was preparing to move out on the right flank to get in a better position to take the enemy under fire, when he suddenly found himself faced with a life-and-death decision. An enemy grenade landed near Powell and Roossien, threatening to kill or injure both men. Without hesitation, Bob Law jumped on the grenade and smothered the blast with his body. He was killed immediately, but his buddies were uninjured.

Enraged by the loss of their friend and fellow Ranger, the rest of the team got up and assaulted the enemy. They quickly destroyed the three VC, then searched their bodies for documents. After they returned to their defensive position, they picked up Bob's body and carried him to a PZ, where they were extracted.

Bob Law displayed the loyalty and commitment that few would ever be known for! John 15:13 reads, "Greater love hath no man than this, that a man lay down his life for his friends." Yes, Bob was really gone, but his memory remains with us eternally.

Bob Law was later awarded the Medal of Honor for his

unselfish sacrifice. It wasn't enough, but he was the first Ranger in Vietnam to receive that award.

Bob Law and Ron Crews stood out as the only two professing Christians that I remembered meeting in the army. It was displayed in their words as well as their deeds. When the chips were down, they shined the light of Christ!

It was a privilege to know and serve with such an outstanding person as Robert D. Law. His name will forever be ingrained in my memory and on an old, black granite wall.

Chapter 37

The Longest Night

On our long journey through life, we go through the good, the bad, and the ugly times. Hopefully, we learn from them all. What I am about to share is the ugliest and "baddest" experience of my life. I have learned things by persevering through this that I hope will be of help to others.

On 23 February, 1969, the North Vietnamese Army began its Second Tet Offensive by attacking several divisional base camps around South Vietnam. We had recently suffered the loss of Bob Law, and my team, Team 1, was still off operational status after Hildebrandt and Lowry were wounded. Our only available teams were few in number and exceedingly busy.

In spite of our limited manpower, Lieutenant Davis was ordered to carry out a special mission by, possibly, none other than the commanding general of the 1st Infantry Division. One team leader had already been given a warning order for this mission; he told the operations sergeant Massey that he preferred not to go because he had a bad feeling about it. Massey informed him that his team was up for the mission unless someone else volunteered. Then, S.Sgt. Enrique Cruz volunteered to take out a team. Since I had just returned from a seven-day leave, I was elected, by a vote of one, to be the point man on the patrol. Staff Sergeant Cruz was assigned four other men to round out the team. Gary Johnson, James Liebnitz, Larry Wenzel, and Robert

Levine were tapped along with me to accompany Cruz on the patrol. These were all dedicated and willing men, but none of us had ever functioned as a team together. After receiving our warning order, we prepared to attend the pre-mission briefing. Before the meeting, we got our rucksacks and equipment ready, and spent the rest of the time trying to get to know one another a little better.

We received some shocking news at the briefing. Intelligence had tracked an overstrength NVA regiment, an estimated four-thousand-plus men from North Vietnam down through Laos and into Cambodia. The latest information put them somewhere near the border of South Vietnam close to an area known as the Fishhook. Our team was to insert northwest of Lai Khe, close to the Cambodian border, about two kilometers just below a part of Cambodia that jutted into South Vietnam and somewhat resembled a fishhook on the map. We were to work an AO in War Zone C to the west of the Song Be Corridor, not far from An Loc. Though we had previously worked in War Zones C and D, as of late, we had been deployed in a lot of short-range patrols around the Lai Khe area.

We were told that the mission was highly classified: our job was to locate the NVA regiment and gather pertinent intelligence about it to send back to operations. The patrol was scheduled to last four days. The AO would contain zero friendlies. Anyone we ran into out there was definitely hostile.

After the meeting ended, we returned to our hootch to discuss specific patrol functions, then finished packing our gear. We got our weapons and double-checked our ammo and grenades. Finally, satisfied with our equipment and individual responsibilities, we waited for Cruz to return from the overflight. We were to insert the next morning

That evening, as we all tried to get a decent night's sleep before the big mission, I felt a sudden, strong urge to get up and write a couple of letters. One was to my stepfather, who had always been like a real dad to me. The other was to my uncle. Both were World War II combat veterans. The two letters were very similar, telling each of them that we were going out on a mission the next day. Since the mission was classified, I couldn't give any of the details, but I had an eerie feeling that we were going to get into some pretty heavy combat, and I told them so. However, I also said that I expected to make it back again. That all seemed so very strange to me, but for some reason I just felt that they would understand. I sealed the letters and took them to the orderly room to mail.

Many facts about the general area that we were to work on this mission were unknown to us. MACV-SOG discovered later that VC and NVA were being supplied from the outskirts of Phnom Penh, Cambodia. Rockets, mortar rounds, and small-arms ammunition came by boat to the seaport of Sihanoukville. Trucks took them on Highway 4 to a depot. From there they were trucked on Highway 7 to the jungle area of Kampong Cham Province, dubbed the Fishhook.

There lay vast stockpiles that supported the 9th Viet Cong division and the 5th and 7th NVA divisions. The Fishhook's largest base contained hundreds of structures, just three miles from South Vietnam.

COSVN, the Central Office for South Vietnam, was the headquarters for all Viet Cong troops in South Vietnam. Its location had been revealed by an NVA turncoat. That strategic camp was only one mile or so inside Cambodia, in the Fishhook. It also housed thousands of transient NVA troops moving into the war zone.

On April 24, 1969, a B-52 Arc Light strike hit COSVN. That was followed by a SOG special operations hatchet force being sent in. The force launched from Quan Loi, a base on Highway 13, just north of Lai Khe. As they landed, the enemy was stirred up like ants coming out of the woodwork. The hatchet force was eaten up by large numbers of NVA troops. Many special forces and their montagnard volunteers were killed or wounded. It was quite sobering to note that so many NVA survived a major Arc Light strike and immediately attacked the hatchet force with a vengeance.

But that all happened just two months *after* our infamous mission. It appeared that we were being sent into an area where maybe as many as forty or fifty thousand or more NVA and VC were encamped. Though we did not know it, we would be working within just a few klicks of that headquarters and enemy stronghold. Most likely the regiment that we were being sent to find probably moved into COSVN to prepare for launching into South Vietnam.

Dawn found us waiting at the chopper pad. We were doing our best to be calm, cool, and collected, but our nerves were on edge, and the usual butterflies were fluttering around in the pits of our stomachs. Cruz motioned us to saddle up. We hopped in the slick and flew off for another jungle excursion.

As Ranger Team Victim Eight, we launched out of Lai Khe, headed for our AO. The electricity raced through the helicopter as we sat looking down at the terrain below, pondering our collective fate. The scenario was much different this time, and our future seemed so uncertain. One would think that after about six months of a steady diet of long-range patrols, I would have become somewhat accustomed to that kind of thing.

The noise caused by the wind blowing through the open cabin made it necessary for us to shout at the top of our lungs to communicate. But that flight, there wasn't any communication—no one had anything to say. We were all victims of a war that no one really understood. We were driven by objectives that had driven young warriors since the dawn of time—youth, courage, ignorance, innocence, bravery, loyalty, insanity—and I wondered which of them was most responsible for my own presence in that unwinding life-and-death drama. What could motivate six young American Rangers to infiltrate into a hostile environment of four thousand enemy soldiers. The absurdity was overwhelming!

I couldn't help but relate our situation, with our lives on the line, to events that were occurring simultaneously back home. Millions were marching against the war and burning the American flag, the flag that we were over there representing with our lives. "There's something happening here—

what it is ain't exactly clear. There's a man with a gun over there, telling me I got to beware." They were only the words from a popular song, but for some reason they seemed to make a lot of sense.

My thoughts suddenly snapped back to the mission as we approached the insertion point. Our pilot made a couple of false insertions, then the third one was the real thing. As point man, I was the first off the helicopter while it briefly touched down in the shallow water of a rice paddy. It was my responsibility to take the lead and get the team into cover. With each member close behind, I jogged a hundred meters across open terrain fully exposed to anyone watching from the nearby cover. With four thousand enemy troops somewhere in the area, I couldn't understand why the pilot had dropped us off so far from the woods. It was a mistake, yet we had no choice but to Charlie Mike. We all expected that trouble wasn't very far away.

When we reached the woods, we discovered a well-used, high-speed trail covered with fresh boot prints. We moved into dense double- and triple-canopy jungle and patrolled very cautiously for an hour or so. Finally, our team leader gave the signal to halt for a much needed break.

As always in that situation, we sat in a circle facing outward, each man watching his assigned area of responsibility. The jungle was steaming at a temperature nearing a humid 105 degrees. And no matter how stealthy we were, we were soon discovered by one of our most insidious enemies—mosquitoes! They were huge and relentless. And soon, their landlocked cousins, the leeches, were joining them in the quest for blood.

Even while being slowly devoured, we had to stay focused or we'd pay the price. But it was sometimes difficult not to step out of reality and let the daydreams in. We would suddenly start thinking about loved ones back home or someday going back to the World, and then we would no longer be mentally alert. The body would still be there, but the mind would be thirteen thousand miles away, grooving with high school chums. Daydreaming killed a lot of young Americans during the Vietnam War. Another popular tune, "Run Through the Jungle," danced in my mind.

After we'd remained put for several hours, listening and resting up, our team leader decided that we were in a good place to RON. He and I went out on a brief recon of the area around us, then returned to the team just before dark. Cruz and I studied the map together, trying to mark our location more accurately. Our last sitrep had us located about a thousand meters to the west and we needed to come up with new coordinates before the next scheduled sitrep. If we got in trouble at night, our people needed to know exactly where we were located.

While the two of us pored over the map, we failed to hear the NVA soldiers who were crawling up to within ten meters or so of our position. The jungle was so thick where we lay hidden that none of us saw, heard, or even anticipated trouble. Suddenly, the enemy opened up on us. The bark of RPD machine guns, AK-47s, and the dull blasts of exploding grenades filled the air with deadly metal. Within seconds, our world had been transformed from a healthy keyed-up silence to a collage of mixed mud, metal, confusion, and blood.

Cruz was killed instantly; a string of machine-gun bullets found his head. The RTO also died in the opening volley, along with his radio, our only means of communication with the outside world. A third team member took several hits in the leg, and his arm was nearly severed. He tried to crawl into the jungle away from the enemy fire, but a grenade exploded nearby and he, too, was killed.

That all happened in the first sixty seconds of the battle. With half the team dead, and the rest of us seriously wounded, we were in a major world of hurt. In just ten seconds, my life had changed forever. One minute, six of us were sitting in a circle in the middle of incredibly dense jungle; the next, three survivors were in a fight for our lives.

Gary was able to return fire as he was being wounded, and it was probably that fact plus the impending darkness that kept the NVA from immediately overrunning us and finishing us off.

I had taken a round through the shoulder and had fallen over Cruz's body. As I tried to crawl away, a machine-gun bullet broke my hip. Then a grenade landed a foot away, exploded, and sent shrapnel into the bullet hole in my hip all the way up into my chest cavity, and almost knocked me unconscious.

I crawled about twenty-five meters from the team and propped myself against a tree. For some reason, the enemy failed to follow up the advantage and pulled back, allowing Larry Wenzel to move over to where I was. He was bleeding from a bullet through his hand and shrapnel wounds in his back. We knew that we were in the biggest trouble of our lives, cut off from help with no radio, and darkness closing in on us.

I tried to get Larry to leave me and return to the original LZ because eventually aircraft would arrive there to search for us. But Larry refused to follow those orders. He simply was not going to leave me alone. But he did go back to the perimeter and carry Gary over to where I was. He also brought along some weapons, ammo, and a first-aid pouch. Gary was already in shock and bleeding internally from multiple bullet and fragment wounds. We bandaged him the best we could, then tended each other's wounds.

Darkness was closing in on us fast. It was the beginning of the longest night of my life. I took out the six fragmentation grenades from my gear. After straightening out the pins, I placed them next to me where I could get to them quickly. We weren't going to be taken prisoner. Suddenly, there were lights penetrating the darkness all around us. The enemy was swarming everywhere with flashlights, trying to flush us. It seemed like there were at least four thousand of them! I knew it would only be a matter of time before they were all over us.

I was barely twenty years old. What was I doing there? I knew that we had a small possibility of survival, so I struggled with my own mortality. I suddenly wondered what we were accomplishing in Vietnam. We could have already won this disastrous debacle if the politicians had let us go on the offensive, instead of having us playing a ridiculous cat-and-mouse game that enabled the enemy to win the war by attrition. It was amazing what goes through your mind when you think you are about to die! I would never see my parents again, never experience the love of a wonderful wife and the joy of having my own children. There would be no career, no growing old. Reality was slapping me in the face!

I heard the choppers looking for us. They were about a thousand meters to the west, but I dared not try to signal them with my strobe light for fear of giving away our position. All we could do was to wait, hope, and pray for some kind of miracle. The helicopters searched for a while and then flew away. At least they knew something had gone wrong. They would put a reaction force in to look for us the next day.

Several times during the night, the NVA passed close by without finding us; finally, they passed on through our position, ushering in quietness. At least, we no longer heard them or saw the flashlights bobbing back and forth among the trees. I couldn't help but wonder if they had really given up, or if they had just decided to lay low and wait until we gave our position away. Or maybe they were waiting to pounce on the reaction force when they arrived. Why didn't they just finish us off and be done with it?

The jungle was a very lonely and terrifying place as we lay out there bleeding, hurting, hungry, thirsty, and scared. Two of my buddies were beside me, blood-soaked and badly wounded. Three others were lying nearby in the jungle, dead. Was it all just some crazy, horrible dream? I knew it wasn't. It was all really happening. I had to keep telling myself that if we could just hang on, the company would surely send someone out to look for us. Don't lose hope, Bill. Don't lose hope.

Pain was coming over me in waves, especially the wound in my hip. My mind was no longer clear. I was beginning to feel confused. Was it because I was losing too much blood, or was it because I was dying? I kept playing different scenarios over and over in my mind, but none of them seemed to play out to an ending where I survived. I fought to overcome fear itself; fear of dying, fear of not being rescued, fear of losing my leg, fear of the unknown, as well as fear of eternity. I kept telling myself that I had not lived long enough; but neither had Wenzel, Levine, Liebnitz, Johnson, and Cruz. Life was so unfair! Then why was I struggling so hard to hold on to it?

During the night, I had to fight to stay awake and to overcome my fears. I knew that the only way to overcome fear of the unknown was to replace it with faith. Faith in God was the key to the whole scenario. I had been remiss in the past, not putting enough faith in the Savior, but out there in the darkened jungle that night, I forced myself to put my trust in Him. I sensed that He was indeed watching over us, protecting us. That was why we were still alive. I focused all my thoughts on Him, placing my faith in the fact that anything that happened from there on out was subject to Him.

As time seemed to stand still, I prayed that night. I thanked the Lord for His mercy and His love. His love was perfect. I remembered that the Bible said that perfect love casts out fear. I asked Him to help me to trust in Him and not be afraid. Christ shedding His blood on the cross reminded me of that unselfish love. His blood was the "war paint" of love that won the greatest battle of all.

The hours dragged on as the pain intensified. Despair, doubt, and death kept knocking at my door, but something deep inside my inner being was determined to survive. The struggle between life and death, between surrender and salvation, continued through the night.

When the steam began to rise from the chilled jungle vegetation, I knew that dawn was not far away. The end of the longest night of my life was at hand. Would it usher in the beginning of the longest day of my life?

As the sky grew lighter, Larry and I prepared to face the inevitable return of the enemy. Just before sunrise we saw seven NVA approach. They were returning to check out the bodies of our teammates and search through our gear. Obviously, the NVA did not feel that there were any survivors around. They kept coming closer as we prepared to strike.

The tables were turned now. Their point man approached

to within ten meters of our position, then stopped, raised his weapon, and began firing into the bodies of our slain teammates. In a blind rage, I opened up on the enemy soldier, but my weapon only fired a single round! I hadn't been aware that my M-16 had been damaged in the ambush the day before. However, that single bullet hit the NVA point man in the neck, killing him instantly.

Joined by Larry, I grabbed a CAR-15 and emptied a magazine at the remaining enemy soldiers. Without waiting to see the outcome of our shooting, I started tossing grenades out into the area where the NVA had been standing just seconds before. One of the frags just happened to hit next to one of our abandoned rucksacks and ignited a smoke grenade.

An LOH scout helicopter searching for us nearby spotted the smoke and buzzed over our position. Somehow, through the thick jungle canopy I was able to get his attention with my signal mirror. He made it clear that he had our location, then turned away and disappeared. Suddenly, it was very lonely again. There was no doubt in my mind that our side was not the only one who now knew where we were. It would be only a matter of minutes before the NVA reappeared. What would they do? Would they attempt to capture us? We couldn't allow that! We had heard too many stories of how they tortured members of special operations teams they took alive. Most likely, the NVA would simply put a hundred or so people on line and merely assault right over us. At least that would get the job done quickly.

But there was still hope that our people would get to us first. A sudden rush of adrenaline coursed through us as our will to survive grew stronger. Someone needed to live to tell what had happened out here, and pass on the intelligence that we had acquired. Desperately, I began to shoot M-79 rounds in a random circle around our position to discourage enemy probes. I didn't really expect the tactic to work, but it was better than doing nothing at all.

Off in the distance we heard the familiar sound of a helicopter. It was coming in at low level. Then it was close to us, and I used my mirror once again to mark our position. He ignored my signal and continued flying grid patterns, searching for us. I was anxious now that he might not find us, and I flashed the mirror in panic.

Then I spotted him! It was a Cobra gunship. He spotted us at the same time. Suddenly, he was right there hovering directly over us. I was overwhelmed by a sudden sense of relief and the feeling that we were going to make it. We were still a long way from being rescued, but at least we had some more friendly company close by. Somehow this made me feel a little more hopeful.

The Cobra pilot, using a cable, began to lower something to us down through the trees. However, he was having a difficult time because of the thick vegetation. Finally, something dropped to the ground not far from our position, and the gunship climbed away from us.

Larry retrieved the package and discovered that it was a PRC-25 radio. Immediately, I got on the air and contacted our people to give them our current sitrep.

More gunships arrived on the scene. I deployed them on firing runs all around our position. With that immediate need taken care of, I requested a medevac helicopter for our wounded and an aerorifle platoon to recover our equipment and our dead.

Soon, an air force pararescue helicopter worked over the top of us and attempted to lower a jungle penetrator down through the trees. But the intertwined branches were so thick that the crew chief was having trouble clearing the vegetation. Just as he was negotiating the worst of the cover, NVA soldiers hiding in the jungle nearby opened fire and caused the pilot to abort the rescue effort. The aircraft took several rounds before it could extract the penetrator and escape the area.

The gunships had to leave to rearm and refuel, and once again we were left behind to contemplate the silence and loneliness of our predicament. The enemy was indeed still out there waiting. It was suddenly clear to us why we had not already been overrun. We were the bait. The enemy obviously awaited our rescue force, so that they could pick them apart. But, who was the enemy anyway? Was it the NVA, the loneliness, the people back home burning our flag, the government who sent us in harm's way with no intention of winning a quick victory, or all of the above?

It was near noon, and I was dizzy and growing very weak. I finally got hold of our support on the radio. "This is Victim Eight. Over."

They responded to my call. Close to passing out from loss of blood, I told them that this would be my last transmission. "Have the ARPs inserted yet?" I inquired.

"Yes," was the reply. "They are three hundred meters away from your position and closing."

Weak, weary, and worn, my mind began to grow cloudy. Larry was talking to me when my world started to spin. Suddenly, a helmet appeared in the bushes not far away. We waved, and the guy under the helmet waved back. The ARPs had found us! They swarmed over us, setting up security all around, and some of them began to hook us up on blood-volume expanders while treating our wounds.

More gunships arrived and began to lay down heavy firepower all around. The pararescue helicopter returned and was finally able to lower the penetrator to us. Gary was unconscious and in bad shape. Larry and I insisted they extract Gary and our dead teammates before we allowed ourselves to be lifted out. Rangers don't leave Rangers behind!

The two of us were hoisted up one by one as enemy bullets flew all around us. Somehow, the chopper pilot managed to lift the overloaded ship out of the jungle and return to Lai Khe. It was just after 1300 hours, nearly twenty hours after we had first been hit. As the chopper touched down on the pad, our fellow Lurps swarmed us. Lieutenant Davis and First Sergeant Cook picked up my stretcher to unload me. I remembered being told that we might be able to return quicker than four days if we got some AKs, so I handed Top an AK-47 and asked if we could come in. Likewise, we'd been told that at least one of us probably would not make it back alive if we performed our mission correctly. How true that turned out to be! Why had they given us the call sign

"Victim Eight"? Why had they inserted us out in the open so far from the woods? Many whys would face Wenzel and me the rest of our lives.

The next day, Larry and I woke up in a MASH hospital. The sick bay around us was full of patients. We inquired about Gary and were informed that our buddy did not survive the surgery. Larry and I were overwhelmed with grief. We had lost four of our teammates—two thirds of an entire patrol. We were the only two survivors—all that was left of our six-man team. Why? How? They were questions that would never find answers. That is why survivors must always live with the memories, the guilt.

Larry Wenzel and Bill Goshen, two young Texans, were finished with their tour of duty, but we both knew that we would be taking Vietnam home with us. We would never forget our fallen teammates. We would never forget Victim Eight. We would never forget the LRPs and Rangers we served with in the 1st Infantry Division. We would never forget the longest night of our lives.

Chapter 38

BAMC 43-C

Wenzel and I barely endured the painful medical evacuation from Lai Khe to Saigon. We spent a few days in a hospital there while the medical staff tried to get us ready for the next leg of our long journey home. My "spica" body cast had to be replaced, because the first one restricted my breathing. The cast encased me like a mummy from chest to my feet.

Finally, the medical staff decided that our conditions had stabilized enough that the two of us could be airlifted to Japan. We arrived at Camp Zama, a couple of pretty sick puppies; we were fighting desperately for our lives. However, that didn't keep us from complaining and haranguing the doctors to ship us back to the States. We weren't the best of patients, but it got the job done. After nine days in Japan, we were carried to a waiting U.S. Air Force jet transport and placed aboard for the long journey back to Travis Air Force Base in California. It was a boring and tedious flight across the Pacific Ocean, but I have to admit that the nurses did a wonderful job trying to keep us comfortable. For an aircraft loaded with badly wounded combat veterans, the flight went relatively well. Only the physical and emotional pain kept the trip from being a welcome and pleasant experience.

After what seemed like days, our plane landed at Travis AFB, not far from Oakland, California. They gave us one night of rest at the hospital there, then put us on another military aircraft to San Antonio, Texas.

On the ground in San Antonio, the walking wounded were put on buses—the rest of us on choppers—for the move to Brooke Army Medical Center at Fort Sam Houston, Texas, near San Antonio. Brooke Army Medical Center was the final destination for thousands of wounded Vietnam vets and was better known to the inmates as BAMC.

Larry Wenzel and I were still together. We were moved into Beach Pavilion and told that it would be our new home for a while. Larry was moved to a ward that specialized in the treatment of hand and arm injuries, while I was wheeled down to Ward 43-C, the orthopedic ward, better known as "broken bones bay." Larry began an ordeal of several operations on his hand. He spent nearly a year at BAMC before the army decided that the best thing it could do for Larry Wenzel would be to medically retire him.

About forty of us occupied the long bay known as 43-C. With the exception of one, we were combat casualties of the Vietnam War. The only non–Vietnam vet was a crusty World War II veteran who suffered greatly from alcoholism and emotional problems. He wore a cast on his leg and banged it on his bed frame a lot. Often, around two in the morning, he moaned and complained about a fish flopping around in his bed. Then he'd start screaming for someone to come and take it away. The ruckus was more than I could endure since I was still plagued with the severe nightmares I had been having all along. Several times I considered crawling out of bed and hushing him up myself. On 43-C, we were all suffering from physical and mental pain, but you had to be a man about it, or at least try. Eventually he was moved away. I hope the poor guy healed from his wounds and was able to go home.

My cast was taken off soon after my arrival. X rays showed my hip was a mess. The doctors' diagnosis was a high proximal fracture of the left femur with multiple grenade fragments in place from my left thigh all the way up into my chest. They drove a stainless steel nail in just under my kneecap and up through the bone to stabilize my leg. The nail protruded from both sides of my leg. When they had finished with the hardware job, they placed me in a new cast, leaving the nail ends exposed. A nylon cord was attached to the nail, and then secured to the bed frame above. This put me in what they termed "a ninety-ninety" traction. My upper leg and knee extended almost vertically, while the lower portion of my leg from my knee down to my foot was forced to lie perpendicular to my upper leg on a horizontal plane. The doctors hoped that keeping me tractioned in that position would allow my hip to grow back together again.

After three and a half *long* months flat on my back, the medical staff rolled in a portable X-ray machine one day to see if the traction had been successful. That was when Lt. Col. Joseph Moll, my orthopedic surgeon, gave me some very alarming news—my hip was not growing back together!

Surgery was mandated. They wheeled me into the operating room and took a bone graft from my right pelvis. The medical team inserted a twelve-inch plate and a Jewett nail along with the bone graft into my left hip, which was necessary if the bone was to grow back together. The enemy machine gun and the grenade had done an effective job of destroying bone and muscle.

The next day, I awoke to find that I was back on 43-C, suffering from a tremendous amount of pain. After a day or two, my sedimentation rate skyrocketed due to a major infection that had invaded my system. The VC and NVA often put substances in their grenades that promoted infection that would often spread through a wounded man like wildfire. It wasn't long before my doctors were talking amputation. I made it a point to let them know, emphatically, that amputation was *not* an option. The doctors countered by telling me that they were only giving me a fifty-fifty chance of survival. Mercifully, I passed out!

The next thing I was aware of was being wheeled down to surgery again. I discovered later that in the course of two weeks, the doctors performed five major operations on me.

Then things began to go from bad to worse! My prognosis was degraded from fifty-fifty to little chance for survival. A day later, I was given no chance for survival as the infection continued to rage through my system. Soon, I was incoherent and next to dead. My parents took a room close by to be with me during these agonizing days.

But back home in the Fort Worth, Texas, area, something very important to my survival was happening. Hundreds of people were praying for me. Members of our fellowship, family, friends, and friends of friends all joined together to offer prayers in my behalf. I later found out that the prayer chain had extended to people outside my neighborhood who had never even known me.

Suddenly, a great miracle began to occur. I regained consciousness and became coherent again. The infection began to subside, and my body began to function better than it had from the time of the wound. None of my doctors could understand the turnaround, but they told me that my chances of survival were good. God's hand was in that. There was no doubt in my mind that I had been the recipient of a God-breathed miracle!

Slowly, my condition continued to improve, until finally the infection was pretty well gone. However, as soon as this threat was eliminated, the next challenge popped up; the doctors informed me that I would probably never walk again, at least not without the aid of crutches. That news devastated me at first, but later it became a challenge.

As the months marched by, I noticed that some of the guys on my ward were being put in wheelchairs and taken down to physical therapy. Others were given crutches and left to hobble around the ward on their own. I began to plead my case for crutches, but for some time the medical staff emphatically refused.

Finally, one day, they brought me a set of crutches and a large belt that went around my waist. The belt was there for someone to hold on to in order to help me keep my balance and prevent me from falling. They also warned me that I would probably pass out the first few steps that I attempted after getting out of bed.

Since I had been hounding them so much about being allowed to walk for exercise, they finally gave in just to show me that it wouldn't work. I sat up in bed and tried to put my feet down, but I was quickly overcome by dizziness. Fighting through the thick fog accumulated during five and one half long months of being bedfast, I shakily stood up on my one good leg. With someone holding the back of my belt, I managed to hobble around the ward on crutches for maybe twenty-five feet and back again. Everyone seemed amazed and pleased. To tell you the truth, so was I!

They started putting me in a wheelchair and rolling me over to physical therapy. At first, I was only able to move my foot and leg a little. After a time I began hobbling around on crutches, and my one good leg. After some adjustments, I could touch the ground lightly with my left foot. A short time later, I could put some pressure on the injured leg. Finally, still on crutches, I began walking, but with a pronounced limp. After a lot of persistence and constant badgering, I finally convinced the staff to drive me to the base swimming pool in an ambulance. I started swimming underwater laps to build up my weak lungs. After a while, I was able to kick a little with my feet as I swam. The day finally arrived when I was able to walk by putting weight on both legs supported by my crutches. That was a very momentous occasion for me. In spite of what the doctors had been telling me, *I could walk!*

After seven major operations and a lot of physical therapy, I graduated to a cane. That may not sound too impressive to most people, but for me, the cane was a new lease on life. It meant that I would be able to get around like a normal human, albeit rather slowly.

The administration began to allow a few of us who were considered ambulatory to leave the base on occasion. Wearing our blue hospital pajamas, we loaded into private vehicles and were driven down to the river walk in downtown San Antonio. By the way people stared at us, I guess we looked a bit bizarre, but we didn't care.

One of our favorite spots was Breckenridge Park. Most Sunday afternoons found us sitting on the grass sipping cold drinks and listening to music on transistor radios. Creedence

Clearwater Revival, the Beatles, the Supremes, and the Temptations blared loudly from our radios as we let the music wash away the horrid memories of the past few months. As The Young Rascals sang "Groovin' on a Sunday afternoon," we struggled to get our lives back together.

A large number of new casualties began arriving on 43-C as others were released to make room for them. Hamburger Hill was the major news item coming out of Vietnam, and we were seeing firsthand the terrible harvest of that operation, during which the Screaming Eagles of the 101st Airborne Division were heavily committed to destroying a major NVA fortified mountain up in I Corps. The casualties were heavy during this multibattalion battle, and many of them were being evacuated to 43-C.

I spent a lot of time visiting the newly wounded, resting at their bedsides, talking to them about what they had just been through, discussing their future prospects, their hopes and dreams, helping them to endure the pain that accompanied the long recovery periods. One of the guys I met was a staff sergeant named Phillip Crow, whose squad had gotten ambushed while moving up the steep slopes of Dong Ap Bia. He was in really bad shape.

That high mountain, situated right on the border between Laos and South Vietnam, overlooked the infamous A Shau Valley, a major enemy stronghold for years. In spite of a number of major operations by the 1st Air Cavalry Division, the Marines, and the 101st Airborne, the NVA were still well entrenched among the valley's surrounding mountains. Dong Ap Bia, or Hamburger Hill, cost us over two hundred KIAs, and another seven-hundred-plus wounded. The enemy lost over two thousand, two hundred soldiers killed, and an unknown number wounded. It was an expensive victory. And when it was over, we pulled out and let them have the mountain back again.

Crow had been hit by shrapnel and had suffered several bullet wounds in the ambush. There was not a lot of hope for his survival. His wife was there, and remained at his side constantly through the long months of his recovery. Phillip

Crow endured many painful operations in his courageous fight for life. With the added strength of his wife's support, he eventually survived the ordeal. So many others didn't!

While I had been in traction, my cast had gained a certain fame around the ward and in the local news media. Many well-wishers had signed their names on it with short messages of encouragement. One popular signature was that of a well-known *Playboy* bunny who had visited the ward. The current Miss America, Judith Ann Ford, had also added her signature to my collection. Brigadier General Moncrief showed up one day to pin a Silver Star on my pajamas, and signed my cast before departing. I was proud to have Larry Wenzel there to stand by me during the presentation. He would later receive a Bronze Star with *V* device, for valor, in a similar ceremony. I felt that his award should have been higher. He was a brave man and a friend.

It would be a flagrant oversight on my part if I failed to mention one particular lady among so many who constantly walked that "extra mile" for all of the wounded vets on 43-C. Mrs. Henry was a jolly, robust, black lady who weighed somewhere around 250 pounds. But she never let her bulk slow her down as she carried on her mission of mercy to "her" wounded vets. We affectionately called her "Mama Cass." That angelic woman went far beyond the call of duty, taking an avid interest in each of the wounded men who lined the walls in 43-C. For some reason, she took a special interest in me, especially during the worst times during my first six months at BAMC. Mama Cass would sit by my bed and talk to me through the worst of the pain, telling me funny anecdotes to help take my mind off the bedsores and the mental anguish of my seemingly hopeless situation. She came back often when she was off duty to bring me a fresh pot of beans and homemade corn bread, or anything else I had a taste for. She kept me from being lonely and gave me hope that someday all of the pain would come to an end. Among the other dedicated volunteers who worked among the wounded, Mama Cass shined like a sparkling diamond. One of the staff members confided that Mama Cass's husband was a casualty in the Korean War. If you read this book, Mama, I still love you.

Christmas, 1969, would always remain very special to us, a most memorable period for all of the vets recovering at BAMC. It was the holiday that Ed Sullivan brought his show live to our bedsides. Entertainers like comedians George Kirby and Marty Allen kept us in stitches (figuratively speaking!). Buck Owens and many others were there, too. But most of us Vietnam vets were most impressed by the presence of that famous female singer, the beautiful Nancy Ames. Wow, did she boost our morale!

All of them were so kind and gracious to us. We had a blast! Mr. Sullivan was especially nice also. They posed for pictures with us and freely signed autographs for all. When the show was over, Ed Sullivan was seen crying on the elevator as he was leaving. They'll never truly understand how much we appreciated their compassion.

After being hospitalized from February 27, 1969, until May 6, 1970, I was medically retired from the U.S. Army at 80 percent permanent disability. My service to my country was over, and I would carry the scars from it both on the outside and inside.

Free of the shackles of hospital confinement, I made the long, tedious drive from San Antonio to Hurst, Texas, in about five hours. I was finally home, at least my body was home. My mind still wandered back and forth from my time at BAMC, to home, and then back to a land thousands of miles across the Pacific Ocean. Vietnam had stamped my soul with an indelible ink. The nightmares came regularly. The experiences I had been through kept replaying themselves in my dreams in living Technicolor. I couldn't get them out of my head.

Bell Helicopter was only a few miles from our home. Every time one of their helicopters flew over the house, I jumped and started to look for cover to hide under. I was like a wild animal, unable to adapt to the cage. I needed time; time and love from my parents and brother and sister.

However, after I was home only five months, an abscess

formed on my left femur. At first it resembled a boil, and it was excruciatingly painful. I called Lieutenant Colonel Moll, my doctor back at BAMC, and told him about this condition. He ordered me to report back to the hospital immediately. So I got into my car and drove back down to San Antonio. When I arrived there, they performed a test on me called a sinogram. This involved injecting some kind of dye into the abscess with a syringe. Then they ran a hose up into my hip and injected more dye the entire time.

After about a year and a half of enduring pain, my tolerance for it was pretty high. But this procedure tapped levels that I had not yet experienced. To make matters worse, they used nothing to deaden the pain. The dye turned a bluish green, signifying that I had developed a bone disease called osteomyelitis. With that affirmed, I was immediately wheeled off to undergo my eighth major surgery. During the procedure, they removed the plate and the nail from my hip, as they were no longer needed for stability. While they were in there, they scraped my femur to remove the osteomyelitis.

I awoke after surgery in a familiar room. I was back in Ward 43-C, my home away from home. There were many new faces there this time, along with a few I recognized. The medical staff informed me that my prognosis looked good. They felt that the osteomyelitis was in the early stages and would probably not return. That sounded good to me. I wasn't looking forward to hitting double numbers in major surgery for a while. However, they wanted me to hang around for a few days to have my stitches removed before going back home.

But I was a civilian then, and the staff could not keep me against my will. So two days later, I decided that I had had enough. The doctors agreed to remove my stitches early; we said our good-byes, and I climbed into my Pontiac LeMans and pointed it toward Fort Worth, Texas, and home.

Chapter 39

Purple Haze

In April 1969, while I was still recovering at BAMC in San Antonio, Texas, our Ranger teams were still in the war back in Vietnam.

Sgt. Barry Crabtree, a team leader, received a warning order for a mission out near the Michelin rubber plantation. His team, composed of Robert Busby, Harry "Frenchy" Suive, and seven other Rangers, was to go in "heavy" on a four-day hunter-killer operation. At the last minute, they decided to take along a pair of M-60 machine guns. After overflying the AO the day before the mission, Crabtree called his team together for a briefing. He informed the men that their patrol was going in on the very edge of the 25th Infantry Division's area of operations. They would be walking off from a 1st Infantry Division firebase and would spend the four days trying to get some "payback" on the enemy.

On the day of the insertion, the team boarded a pair of slicks and flew out to the friendly firebase. At first light the next day, they walked out of the perimeter and disappeared into the surrounding vegetation.

A short time later, they discovered a high-speed trail covered with Ho Chi Minh sandal tracks. The team continued moving parallel to the trail, keeping to the jungle along its flank.

Just before dark, Crabtree decided to set up an ambush

on the trail during the evening. After putting out a number of claymore mines in strategic locations, the team crawled back into some nearby cover and concealment to await the enemy.

Crabtree assigned the men to watches and told those not on guard to try to get some rest. Nothing unusual happened during the night. But as daylight approached and the team came awake, Crabtree discovered fresh tracks all over the trail. The enemy had come through them while the team had been on watch, yet no one had seen a thing. Crabtree suspected that someone had fallen asleep on watch, but no one would claim responsibility or admit to having seen anything during his guard shift. Apparently from the tracks, the VC had traveled up a nearby creek in a sampan. They had jumped out onto the trail and conducted some business nearby. When they had finished, they climbed back aboard their sampan and left.

There were several new men on the patrol, and Crabtree suspected that one of them had dozed off instead of watching the trail. Something that stupid could get a team wiped out in a heartbeat. Crabtree admonished the entire team and ordered them to proceed with the mission. He decided to take the point himself and go in search of the enemy.

During that day, Crabtree made a serious mistake and crossed over into the 25th Infantry Division's area of operations. That evening the patrol once again set out their claymores in an ambush configuration and started to settle in for the night.

Immediately, four NVA soldiers appeared on the trail walking directly toward the team. The NVA were wearing pith helmets with metal gold bars on them. Ten meters away from the team, the four NVA entered the kill zone, then suddenly turned away. Believing that the enemy had spotted them, Crabtree blew his claymore, initiating the ambush. One of the NVA was wounded in the initial blast and began screaming at the top of his lungs. The rest of the team blew their claymores, and Busby threw several grenades out into the kill zone to seal their escape and three NVA were killed instantly. When the Rangers checked out the bodies, they discovered that they were officers or senior NCOs.

Suddenly, Busby screamed, "Grenade!" Crabtree dropped behind his rucksack as the grenade exploded. Busby was lying on his back wounded. Crabtree crawled over to his M-16 and discovered that the weapon had been mangled by the shrapnel and was useless. He then crawled over to Busby and found that he was unconscious and already going into shock. His lips were beginning to turn blue.

The enemy grenade set off a purple smoke grenade on Crabtree's rucksack, blinding the team as the smoke swirled around. Everything was hidden in a thick purple haze that hung stationary in the air amid the heavy vegetation. Crabtree quickly got on the radio and called Captain Hansen, the Ranger company commander, to report the contact. When he asked for a medevac and gave Hansen the team's coordinates, he discovered that they were out of their AO. Hansen told them that they were in the 25th's AO, and ordered them to move back to their own immediately. Crabtree threw Busby over his shoulder and followed the team back to where they were supposed to be. They located an old earthen berm and circled up in a defensive position, calling for Cobra gunships to support them. Crabtree had no idea what they were facing, but he wasn't taking any chances. Busby was bleeding internally, and they had to get him out quickly if he was to survive.

Gunships began firing up the surrounding area as the team began taking sporadic fire from the enemy. With a critically wounded man on his hands and an unknown enemy force around them, Crabtree realized that they were in over their heads and requested an infantry company to come to their support. The grunts soon arrived and continued the contact. A medevac came in and evacuated Busby to the closest MASH hospital. A short time later, extraction ships arrived and took out the rest of the team. Robert Busby survived his wounds and was later evacuated to a hospital back in the United States. He had served his unit well and would be sorely missed.

Sometimes simple missions became amazing adventures. Some ended on a positive note, some killed young men and left gaping wounds on the bodies and minds of those who survived. Crabtree's had become a "purple haze" of confusion, and wound up with another Ranger wounded in action.

Chapter 40

The Quan Loi Fiasco

The following month, the company inserted two recon teams out of Quan Loi base camp. They were working adjacent AOs about seven kilometers outside the base camp near the Cambodian border. Sgt. Barry Crabtree's team detected enemy movement right after clearing the insertion LZ. The terrain they were operating in consisted of farmland and rubber plantations, broken up here and there by small tracts of jungle. The team moved slowly and cautiously away from the LZ, but soon began taking sporadic RPG fire from a distance. They could not locate the enemy, but each time they tried to move, more RPG fire was directed at them.

They had moved into an area dominated by elephant grass, making visual observation of their surroundings almost impossible. They detected more movement around them and called in a revised situation report. A colonel back in the rear got on the radio and told Crabtree to remain where he was while the other team, led by Sgt. Bob Roossien, moved in to link up with them.

During that time, Crabtree's team had never been more than seventy-five meters from their original insertion point. The enemy was all around them, and apparently in large numbers. In spite of that, the two Ranger teams managed to link up.

Moving out, they crossed a trail in the elephant grass, and two enemy soldiers suddenly appeared fifty meters away and began shouting at them. The NVA appeared to be taunting the Rangers. Crabtree sensed that they were being baited to open fire, giving away their numbers. It was getting dark, and wisely, nobody opened fire. They moved a few meters away and circled up into a defensive perimeter.

The elephant grass around them was so thick and high that the Rangers knew they would soon be in a no-win game of hide-and-seek with the enemy. According to his map, Crabtree understood there was a clearing not far away. The Rangers agreed among themselves to escape and evade toward the clearing if the enemy found them during the night.

Out in the middle of the elephant grass, the Rangers discovered a large hole formed by an old rubber tree stump that had rotted away. The craterlike hole was just big enough for all ten Rangers to gather in the depression, shoulder to shoulder. There they waited quietly to see what the enemy was up to. As it got darker, the enemy sent two men out on the flanks of the elephant grass to climb trees and hold flashlights over their heads. Using the two beacons as reference points, the gooks got on line and began moving away from the Ranger's positions in the direction of nearby Quan Loi. Sending a man up a tree to observe, the Rangers estimated that there were between four and five hundred enemy troops on the move. Then it started to rain.

Crabtree got on the radio and called Quan Loi to warn them of the situation. The same unknown colonel got on the phone and asked the team leader to repeat his message. When Crabtree was finished, the colonel refused to believe him. The two men had a heated discussion about the team's report, but the information was not heeded.

Suddenly, there was more movement in the grass around the teams as enemy troops swept through the place. The Rangers called in artillery in an attempt to keep the enemy away from their position. The rounds came dangerously close, and shrapnel and large pieces of debris began falling into their tight perimeter.

The enemy began moving through the grass in smaller,

scattered groups. Suddenly, one of the groups came too close, and the Rangers were forced to fire them up. The enemy did not return fire, then everything became quiet. It remained so for the rest of the night.

At first light, Crabtree's team discovered that the grass had been matted down all around them. Apparently, his team had inserted right into the middle of an enemy unit staging point preparing for an attack on Quan Loi. It was incredible that any of them were still alive!

Suddenly, about twenty-five enemy soldiers broke out of the grass running toward the team's position. The Rangers opened fire and the enemy dispersed. Again, the enemy failed to return fire.

Crabtree had experienced enough of the cat-and-mouse game. He called for an aerorifle platoon, and after a short wait, the help was inserted nearby. The Rangers linked up with the aerorifle platoon on some high ground nearby, and Crabtree informed their platoon leader about what had transpired. With the aerorifles securing the high ground, the Rangers moved down the hill and quickly spotted another group of enemy soldiers.

Suddenly, Bob Roossien took a round in the chest and fell to the ground next to Newcombe and Crabtree. He was dead by the time they dropped down to check him. Another Ranger was wounded seconds later, taking a bullet in the ankle. Up on the hill behind them, the aerorifle platoon remained in place and failed to come to their aid.

The Rangers killed a couple of enemy soldiers and searched their bodies, confiscating papers and weapons. Fearing a trap, the Rangers picked up their dead and wounded and climbed back up the hill to the aerorifle platoon's location. Together they walked back into the Quan Loi perimeter. Later that day, the surviving Rangers were flown back to Lai Khe.

It appeared that the good colonel ignored the early warning called in by our Rangers. His refusal to believe their eyewitness account of the enemy outside his location resulted in Quan Loi being assaulted and partially overrun the following night. We lost Bob Roossien, and another man was wounded and shipped home, for nothing. Our early warning had been turned into a fiasco. Bob had been an outstanding Lurp-Ranger as well as a fine individual. He would be impossible to replace all because of a humbug mission and an irresponsible colonel.

Chapter 41

The Long Road Back

An old saying became a new reality for me. Namely, the third time is the charm, which is better than three strikes and you are out. In high school, I dated a girl named Pam. At the time, we became serious and informally engaged. Then, I moved on to college, and she moved on to one of her old boyfriends and ended up marrying him.

Next, just after becoming a civilian again, along came a blonde named Donna. We dated awhile and became formally engaged. That didn't last too long, either.

Not long after my return home, my life suddenly took a major turn for the better. Back during my senior year in high school, Jackie Coble was in the seventh grade. But by the time I had returned from my military service, she had grown into a beautiful lady. What a difference four years makes!

The year was 1970, and there was a lot of unrest on local school campuses and elsewhere throughout the nation. However, a seventeen-year-old high school senior caught up in her small-town, teenage world, rarely considered all these nationwide and worldwide concerns of war and peace. Her U.S. history studies never really covered beyond the Korean War because of a lack of time at the end of the year. So she had no understanding of the Vietnam fighting whatsoever. The war was a hazy picture of something far removed across the world. The newsreels flashed a blur of soldiers not personally known to her. They were there—she was here. (A world apart, it seemed.) Her father had not been a military man because of health problems. She had no brothers. Only a second cousin had been in Korea and Vietnam.

But something happened to permanently change her focus, to awaken her to the reality of the war, and to gain a respect for the soldiers fighting there for freedom. When a twenty-two-year-old Vietnam veteran came into Jackie's life, things drastically changed. That veteran was me. According to her, my character was much different from the average—gentle, but at the same time that of a physically well-built, strong-tempered soldier. My underlying hurts and outward scars gave a realistic picture of my near-death encounter in Vietnam and of my sixteen months in the hospital at Fort Sam Houston.

She was intrigued by me because my experiences far exceeded hers. My wounds and losses of friends in the war were fresh memories, and often, clad in my cut-off army fatigue shirts, I shared them with her. Her heart reached out, seeking to alleviate the turmoil within me. For by then, she had grown to love me. But in her innocence, how could she soothe my inner wounds? Outwardly I seemed tender, but inside, my heart was a keg of dynamite! What would it take to disengage the inner time bomb? In the midst of the emotional travail, however, we became engaged. We married on April 7, 1972. That nineteen-year-old girl matured fast. She was confused, and I was at the end of my rope in despair.

Thankfully, before it was too late, our lives changed directions. Realizing I had no power within myself to overcome this hopeless lifestyle, I submitted my life to the one who was more than capable to carry me through. Sometimes the emotional anguish surfaced, but now I had hope. I began focusing on the "Healer of hurts" to be my strength. In addition, the emptiness in her life was filled by Jesus Christ. Now our new adventure began to unfold. I started the process of accepting the fact that my life had been spared for a purpose. Therefore, I needed to speak often of God's mercy and grace in sparing my life and allowing me to walk again. I needed to proclaim his love and forgiveness along with the new life He brings.

Throughout the upcoming years, there were numerous re-unions with old army friends. Jackie learned that she had to make room for those special relationships. Because of the camaraderie of fellow soldiers, our hearts were knit together in brotherly love. She realized that she was not being ex-cluded. These meetings provided opportunities to support, encourage, and understand. They were my common link to the past, while she became my friend and teammate of today.

Jackie and I became one, best friends, and a team. She walked side by side with me through the good times as well as the emotionally difficult ones; she earned her stripes as a real trooper. We were very blessed with two wonderful chil-dren. Our daughter, Wendy, came into our lives in October of 1974. Then, in September of 1978, our son, Kurt, arrived on the scene. Our children inspired us to remain united even in the hard times. They brought joy when gloom tried to ap-pear. We had moved from two people to a five-person team—Bill back on point, Jackie as RTO, Wendy at slack, Kurt at rear security, and Jesus Christ as team leader.

The monumental event in my life took place in March of 1975. Haunting memories and lack of sleep finally took their toll. I was dealing with the common things that combat vets must face, but I was also facing a deeper spiritual problem. Yes, I knew about Christ and his sacrifice for our sins, but I did not know Him personally as my Lord and Savior. It was on the second of March that I called out to Him to forgive me and come into my life. Immediately, things started get-ting better; problems still existed, but now He was with me. A process of healing and restoration began in Bill Goshen. *Jesus became real in me!*

To those of you who have suffered the horrors of combat, whether it was World War II, Korea, Vietnam, Grenada, Cen-tral America, Desert Storm, Somalia, or some other place, know and understand that your sacrifices have registered both in heaven and earth. You are appreciated by many, even though at times you may not feel like it.

In diverse ways, this great republic of ours endures many threats and assaults on it. Our wonderful Constitution and

Bill of Rights are sometimes swept under the rug by greedy politicians without moral character, but both are still very much alive. They continue to exist and thrive in the hearts of many despite momentary attacks on them.

A democratic government can only be as good as those who are governed. Greed and deception constantly battle to replace compassion and truth. Maybe it is a good time for all of us to consider what legacy we will leave for those who come after us. Will they be able to say that we did a good job? Will we be scorned and vilified for destroying their inheritance?

War paint is a symbolic, external sign of impending combat. When American Indians applied it to their faces and bodies, it meant that they were ready to launch into battle. As LRPs, when we painted our faces, it signified that we were once more preparing to do battle with our enemies.

However, the greatest warrior of all allowed His body to be broken on a cross at a place known as Mount Calvary. His war paint was His precious Blood. The Blood of the Lord Jesus Christ flowed down His body, paying the heavy price for our sins.

By doing that He defeated the greatest enemies of all—death and eternal damnation—so that we might live forever at peace with Him and ourselves.

Isaiah 53:4-6 tells us that Jesus bore our grief and our sorrow. He was wounded for our transgressions and bruised for our iniquities. He was chastised for our peace; by His stripes we were healed. We all go astray in sin, but God laid on Christ Jesus all our iniquities.

Not everyone may agree with my Christian principles or my covenant with my Savior, but my faith has strengthened me and given me the courage and the faith to go on with my life. It has helped me to place my experiences in Vietnam where they belong. I cannot live in the past, but I shall not forget. I won't forget the ones I served with and the price they paid.

I certainly do not claim to be a hero. Larry Wenzel and I are survivors of a terrible war that we will never forget. I still love the United States of America and our grand old flag. Freedom is precious, and it carries a price tag that most people are ignorant of. May freedom always clothe our children and their children with its mantle of beauty.

George Washington made a statement that is certainly appropriate here. He stated that it is impossible to rightly govern the world without God and the Bible. The United States of America has a major choice to make, return to Christ or pay the price.

Romans 10:9–10 (NLT) says, "For if you confess with your mouth that Jesus is Lord and believe in your heart that God raised him from the dead, you will be saved. For it is by believing in your heart that you are made right with God, and it is by confessing with your mouth that you are saved."

Chapter 42

Smorgasbord

Warfare, by its very nature, deals with the pains of people. This is wrong! People hurting other people is traditional nonsense. The Bible tells us to treat others the way we want them to treat us. It is a sad commentary on human morality that modern society cannot adhere to that golden nugget of wisdom. In order for people to coexist, law and order must prevail; the antithesis will certainly be anarchy. Punishment of evildoers and violators of those laws is necessary for society to remain free and at peace. If the justice system is not just, it must be changed. If it is not changed in a correct manner, and the reforms put into practice, then we are doomed. War and rebellion will always erupt when the oppressed have finally suffered enough.

Vietnam is a classic example of what can happen when the common people are treated unjustly and have had "enough." Part of the population rebels and chooses sides. Outside forces get involved, escalating the unrest. War breaks out and those in the middle, which always comprise the majority of the populace, suffer from the violence that ensues. Mankind must learn to work out its differences in better ways, or we will continue to pay the price in blood.

In August 1997, the former LRRP/LRP/Rangers of the 1st Infantry Division came together for a three-day reunion.

Some brought their wives and children. We visited a lot of the local attractions, and enjoyed the fellowship. There were a few war stories exchanged—that's only natural—but most of the conversations were about our families, jobs, current affairs, post-traumatic stress disorder, and future reunions. However, the conversations always seemed to shift back to those years so long ago, and a land with so much pain and sorrow.

I maintain a strong brotherly love for all my former comrades from the war. We have a devotion to one another that is difficult to explain, and impossible to sever. The crucible of fire that we survived links our lives together permanently. We must all deal with those memories, good and bad. May we live in the present, for the future, and may we truly learn from the past.

The following includes parts of some conversations that took place at the '97 reunion: retired sergeant major John Tapia LRP'd with us on several teams and later served as a team leader. He also served as a platoon sergeant and sergeant first class with our unit. Tapia recalls many things that happened in our company. One was about our company mascot, a dog we called Zulu. Zulu liked to visit guys while they enjoyed their beer; someone always gave him a little. That only encouraged him to beg for more, and LRPs, being by nature very generous and giving people, would always comply. Soon Zulu would be running around in circles, getting dizzier and dizzier until he finally passed out. He would awake much later with a monster hangover and stay in a foul mood until it went away. In a sense, Zulu was a lot like many of the LRPs in our company. Those were "dog days" for a lot of us.

Sgt. Lyn Caig remembered a harrowing mission in November 1967. Back then, the LRRPs were attached to Headquarters, 1st Infantry Division, working mainly out of Lai Khe. On that particular mission, Caig's team was to make a last-light insertion out near the always dangerous Hobo Woods. Two montagnard scouts were to walk double-point for the eight-man patrol. George Knowlton was the team leader, with Elsner the ATL. Sorick and two other LRRPs rounded out the team.

The choppers landed on the helipad and picked up the LRRPs. Everyone anticipated just another excursion into the enemy's lair. As they approached the LZ, it was almost dark. The two 'yard scouts jumped off first with the rest of the team right on their heels. They wagon-wheeled and listened for sound of the enemy. After getting a good commo check and releasing the choppers, the team moved out with the two scouts in the lead. Knowlton sensed that they seemed to be moving a little too fast. He and his LRRPs could hardly keep up. After an hour or so, the team lost contact with the point element. The two 'yards were nowhere to be found.

Suddenly, the silence was shattered by the sounds of explosions and gunfire. They had walked into an ambush. The team was pinned down and unable to move. They quickly called in artillery and began walking it all around the perimeter. That forced the enemy back, but it was too dangerous to attempt to get helicopters in during the night to extract the team, so they had to hold out until dawn.

George Knowlton and two other LRRPs had been hit in the opening fire. George had suffered a sucking chest wound and was dying. Flying high overhead, the company commander in the command-and-control aircraft was in constant communication with the team. He ordered the patrol to move from their location, but the enemy was everywhere. Elsner refused to leave Knowlton and the other wounded behind. He said that he was the commander on the ground, and it was his decision to make.

Finally, dawn began to break over the patrol. Knowlton had died during the night. Medevac helicopters reached the team and evacuated two other wounded LRRPs and rushed them to the nearest hospital. Elsner and the other survivors were extracted and taken back to Lai Khe, where they were notified that they were relieved of duty pending a court-martial. Amazingly, they were charged with disobedience in the face of the enemy.

The team was finally cleared of all charges and reported back to duty. That event led to a policy among the Big Red One's LRRPs that the team leader on the ground had the final say. No one flying high above a team in trouble on the ground was in a position to make a life-and-death judgment without being there. Besides, in the case at point, Elsner was also following the established tradition that all LRRPs lived by: LRRPs never leave LRRPs behind.

Chapter 43

Feelings

My story will not be complete without a few miscellaneous comments. I am truly proud and honored to say that I served as a member of the U.S. Army long-range patrols and Rangers.

Today, the 75th Ranger Regiment contains the finest fighting men in the world. After meeting many of them at LRRP/LRP/Ranger reunions at Fort Benning, Georgia, I am absolutely convinced that they are on the cutting edge of combat readiness. My hopes and prayers remain that they will never have to launch into combat again, but I sleep well with the knowledge that if they ever do, they will be ready, willing, and more than able. Hooah!

The men who served in combat during the Vietnam War continue to pay a very heavy price for their participation. The men who served on behalf of the 1st Infantry Division with F Company, 52d Infantry (LRP) and Company I, 75th Infantry (Ranger), suffered a greater relative aggregate of casualties than any other LRRP/LRP/Ranger company in the Vietnam War. The long-range patrollers and Rangers of the 101st Airborne Division lost the most men, but they served in Vietnam for a longer period of time.

Many believed that our tremendous loss of men resulted from being under the command of a far too aggressive 1st Infantry Division operations section. Others felt the cause of such loss was simply heavy combat. Both may be true. No one could know for sure.

But I can say with complete confidence that the long-range patrollers of the Big Red One definitely served valiantly, daring to walk point as the eyes and ears of the 1st Infantry Division. Let it be known to all that we shall continue the mission for ourselves, and for family, friends, and freedom. "LRRPs never leave LRRPs behind!" So, keep on LRPin' for this republic, because our children will live with the results.

The Last Team

by Bill Goshen

Hello, America! How goes it for you?
Yes, it's me calling again . . . To the red, white, and blue!
Does Old Glory still fly? Does freedom still ring?

Hello, people of the United States! Please tell me what's
   new.
Are the Beatles still popular? And Elvis Presley, too?
How's my '68 Vette . . . the one I bought new!?
Hello, Mom and Dad . . . are you still alive, too?

Hello, my fellow countrymen and my Commander in Chief.
The days are so lonely with heartaches and grief;
I spend much time remembering things I used to do.
Sally, are you still waiting . . . or have you forgotten, too?

It might not be so bad here with clothing and shoes
Some decent food and medicine and someone to talk to!
Oh, I still tap out messages to the Lurp next door
And to the pilot on the other side, but tapping's a bore!

May I ask just one question, just so I will know?
Why have you left us here these last thirty years or so?
We gave our very best from the DMZ, Phu Bai, and Da
   Nang,
From Sa Dec to Lai Khe to the Iron Triangle and Nha Trang!

Please forgive us for being so emotional expressing our
feelings this way,
But I heard two guards talking about normalized relations
with the USA.
They conversed about burying us alive with all others
they've detained.
Why didn't they do it years ago and save us all this shame?

Though the guns be silent—no more choppers coming to
save
No more—Breaker One Niner Savoy—no more fire missions to stage.
What's that you're saying, Mr. President? We're the highest
priority today!
If our country waits much longer—nobody will be left to
save!

What is that outcry in our land? We want our brothers home
from Vietnam;
Down with normalizing with Communists we say
Bring them home alive—bring them home today!

Breaker Breaker—this is Victim Eight to whomever our
president may be,
This is the last team waiting for extraction from the land of
our enemy.
Is that really you on this frequency, Mr. President?
Who are we, you say?

Why—we are the Last Team in Vietnam—LRPS, Rangers,
SEALs, and the Green Berets!
We're Pilots, Infantry, Marines, Artillery, all that defended
liberty's way.
Who are we you say—America?!
We're the forgotten, the POWs and MIAs.

Echoes of Freedom

by Bill Goshen

Hello there, USA—Land of the Free
And home of the brave;
Listen to your history today,
Sounding from the graves!

Hear the echo of the cavalry troopers
And the songs of the Indian braves,
We both fought with much courage
Our blood for your heritage.

From another chapter of American history
Did a different battle rage,
Known painfully as the Civil War
With General Lee and Honest Abe!

From Shiloh to Vicksburg, blood was shed
Every engagement left many men dead;
Bull Run, Richmond, and Chancellorsville, too;
We died wearing gray, and we died wearing blue.

Then came the carnage of World War I
From the Marne River to the siege of Verdun;
From the Argonne Forest to the battles at sea
The price ran high for your liberty.

Then came the big one, called World War II
A day of infamy for the red, white, and blue;
We fought at Bataan and Omaha Beach,
Anzio, Japan, then Germany . . . we reached.

The cost ran high to win this global fight
We died in trenches and jungles day and night;
Both subs and sharks caused us watery graves
Our sacrifices recorded on history's page.

Next came Korea—thousands did go
We fought in bitter winter—in rain and snow;
Merely a conflict in our leaders' eyes,
Thousands became widows as we husbands died!

From Seoul to the Yalu River and the 38th parallel, too
We bled, we froze, and we fought for you;
An undeclared war—a mere conflict you see
Freedom's price was high—we're your history!

Next in our archives is one Vietnam
On the other side of the world we flew,
From Sa Dec to Lai Khe, on to the DMZ
Through rice paddies and jungles, too.

Listen to the echoes at Hamburger Hill
To the cries of the infantry slain,
To the SEALs, Lurps, and Rangers, too
Marine Recon, and the Green Beret!

Many say we lost the war
That "Charlie" was too tough to beat;
Had our government allowed us to fight offensively
Hanoi would have fallen in defeat.

We proved in Grenada, what we could do
Over in Panama, too;

Then, came Desert Storm where we flexed our might
And waved "Old Glory" for you!

Listen to your heritage, as we cry from the grave
Always remember freedom's cost;
Train up your children to understand, too,
Lest you find your freedom lost!

Turn back America to the red, white, and blue;
And raise "Old Glory" high;
Go back to your roots—embrace your heritage,
Lest you find that freedom died!

Postscript

Living in peace is certainly an admirable objective. In a world filled with much anger, greed, and selfishness, peace is only temporary at best!

I have found that only the Prince of Peace can give me real peace even in the midst of the storm. The greatest warrior ever is the Lion of the tribe of Judah, Jesus Christ. He has won the war of the ages on the cross and did it with love. Love never fails.

—John 11:25–26

Appendix A

Statistics of United States Wars

WAR	DURATION	MEN ENGAGED	DEAD	PCT
American Revolution	8 years	250,000	4,000	2.6
War of 1812	2 yrs. 7 mos.	528,000	2,000	.3788
Mexican War	1 yr. 5 mos.	116,600	13,000	11.15
Civil War*	4 yrs. 1 mo.	2,129,000	497,821	23.383
Spanish-American	4 mos.	280,500	2,446	.872
World War I	1 yr. 7 mos.	4,355,000	116,000	2.66362
World War II	3 yrs. 8 mos.	15,272,000	406,000	2.65846
Korean War	3 yrs. 1 mo.	1,200,000	54,246	4.520
Vietnam	9 yrs. 5 mos.	3,108,000	57,685	1.856
Persian Gulf War	43 days	540,000	268	.004964
TOTAL	43 yrs. 7 mos.	26,368,100	1,211,151	4.59325

*Union side only; Confederate figures unavailable

Appendix B

Vietnam War
Killed in Action, LRPs and Rangers of the 1st Infantry
  Division

HQ and HQ Co. LRRPS—1st Infantry Division
CO. F, 52d Infantry, LRPS
CO. I 75th Infantry Rangers
Our 27 Valiant Ultimate Sacrifices

1.	Sgt. Rudolph A. Nunez	13 Jun. 66
2.	S.Sgt. George F. Knowlton	19 Nov. 67
3.	Sgt. James P. Boyle	17 Apr. 68
4.	S.Sgt. Jack G. Liesure	12 May 68
5.	Pfc. Edward Carson	21 Oct. 68
6.	Sgt. William P. Cohn, Jr.	21 Oct. 68
7.	Pfc. Gerard Coyle	21 Oct. 68
8.	Sp4. Lester A. Doan	21 Oct. 68
9.	Pfc. Steven Sorick	21 Oct. 68
10.	Pfc. Jim A. Boots	13 Nov. 68
11.	Pfc. James Blume	21 Nov. 68
12.	Pfc. Arnold L. Mulholland	21 Nov. 68
13.	S.Sgt. Anthony F. Washington	21 Nov. 68
14.	Sp4. Reynaldo Arenas	31 Dec. 68
15.	Sp4. Robert D. Law	22 Feb. 69

16. S.Sgt. Enrique S. Cruz   27 Feb. 69
17. Sp4. Robert P. Levine   27 Feb. 69
18. Sp4. James T. Liebnitz   27 Feb. 69
19. Pfc. Gary L. Johnson   28 Feb. 69
20. Sgt. Anthony G. Markovitch   16 Apr. 69
21. Sgt. Robert A. Roossien   12 May 69
22. Capt. Reese M. Patrick   14 May 69
23. Sp4. Charles E. Smith, Jr.   18 Aug. 69
24. Sgt. Bernard A. Propson   05 Sep. 69
25. Pfc. Michael Randall   21 Oct. 69
26. Sgt. Mike R. Kernan   25 May 70
27. S.Sgt. Timothy V. Harper   17 Feb. 71

NOTE: This is the best list we could get. If anyone was excluded, please forgive us.

Appendix C

KIA Dedication

Our wonderful National Anthem echoes over every state of the union, "The land of the free and the home of the brave . . ." Consider, our land would not be a land to live in freedom if it were not for the brave!

Freedom carries a very costly price tag for its birth and preservation. White crosses in cemeteries in every state are solemn reminders of the blood shed for our freedom.

From our war for independence well over two hundred years ago, blood continues to be the payment for the citizens of the United States of America to make choices others cannot. May we always remember that indeed all that have served in our Armed Forces gave some, but *some gave all*!

The following symbol and meaning were created by Ken and Ramona Peck, Mike and Merle Dinoto, David and Bernice Calhoun, and Bill and Jackie Goshen in honor of those killed in action from all wars we have fought since our nation's birth!

The KIA Symbol

KIA means killed in action, and red symbolizes the blood they shed! Green olive branches stand for peace. The green grass with white crosses represents their graves and are a solemn reminder of freedom's price. The bald eagle is the symbol of the United States of America. The eagle also represents the KIAs who were once young eagles strong and brave. The eagle is flying off into eternity having conquered death. He carries the golden cross of eternal life. The golden circle reminds us of the selfless love these young eagles displayed for America and Americans. This circle also suggests that we remember the never-ending love of God! Our military and law enforcement keep us from harm's way; outlaws from within and foreign powers must consider the cost for their offenses! The blue peaceful sky of our nation houses no enemy fighters or bombers to do us harm. Likewise, our homes and streets are relatively safe for us, because *some gave all*! They died for us to live in peace and freedom! The sun shines its bright rays of hope for the future. Remember, America, freedom demands maintenance. The royal blue background of this symbol along with the red KIA and white *V* stand for the colors of our National Flag and the victory we have when united. The golden background of the flag is to remind us that the United States of America is a land of golden opportunity both for immigrant and native. The entire symbol warns our adversaries of our determination and points us back to our Constitution, lest we crumble from within.

SOME GAVE ALL

KIA

Yellow	Red
Light blue	Green
Gold	Blue

Glossary

A-1 Skyraider: Korean War–vintage, propeller-driven fighter-bomber, a SOG favorite because of its heavy payload, long loiter time, and precision ordance delivery.

AA: Antiaircraft.

AC: Aircraft commander, pilot.

A camps: Border surveillance camps manned by U.S. Special Forces–led mercenaries, to detect infiltrating NVA units. SOG sometimes launched cross-border operations from A camps.

Acid pad: Flat, hard-surfaced area designed to accommodate helicopter landings and takeoffs.

AFVN: Armed Forces radio and TV network—Vietnam.

Air burst: An explosive device, such as a grenade, a bomb, an artillery round, or a mine, rigged to detonate above the ground to inflict maximum damage by expanding the range of shrapnel.

Air-conditioning: An artificial temperature-control device, widely used by army rear echelon and air force personnel, said to establish and maintain living conditions similar to those found in civilian life in the continental United States.

Air strike: Surface attack by fixed-wing fighter-bomber aircraft.

AIT: Advanced individual training following basic combat training.

AK-47: Communist fully automatic assault rifle.

AO: Area of Operations. A defined geographical area where military operations are conducted for a specific period of time.

Ao dai: Traditional Vietnamese female dress, split up the sides and worn over pants.

ARA: Air rocket artillery. Military description of Huey gunships.

Arc Light: B-52 bombing mission.

Article 15: Punishment under the Uniform Code of Military Justice. Less severe than general courts-martial.

Artillery fan: Area within range of supporting artillery.

ARVN (ARVIN): Army of the Republic of Vietnam.

ATL: Assistant team leader. Second in command on a LRP or Ranger team.

AWOL: Absent without leave.

BCT: Basic combat training. Initial course of training upon entry into the United States Army.

BDA: Bomb damage assessment. A special operations mission for the purpose of verifying results of an aerial bombing attack.

Beaucoup: French for "very many."

Beehive: An anti-personnel artillery round containing thousands of small darts or fléchettes.

Berm: High, earthen levee surrounding most large, permanent U.S. military installations as part of the perimeter defense system.

Big Red One: Slang used to denote the First Infantry Division.

Black box: Sensor devices planted along trails, roads, rivers, and at intersections and junctions to detect body heat, perspiration, or sound given off by passing enemy troops.

Blasting cap: The detonator inserted into claymore mines, grenades, satchel charges, and other explosive devices, which initiates the actual detonation.

Blood trail: Spoor sign left by the passage or removal of enemy wounded and dead.

Blue line: Designation on maps of streams, rivers, and other natural waterways.

Body bag: Rubberized canvas or plastic bags used to remove dead U.S. casualties from the field to Graves Registration locations.

Body basket: A wire litter lowered by cable from a medevac helicopter to aid in the evacuation of critically wounded personnel, where landing is impossible because of terrain conditions.

Boonies: Informal term for unsecured areas outside U.S. control.

Boozers: Slang term for military personnel who frequently indulge in heavy alcoholic consumption.

Bush: Informal term for the jungle, also called boonies, boondocks, Indian country, or the field.

Butter Bar: Second lieutenant.

C-3 or C-4: Plastique explosives.

CA: Combat assault.

CAR-15: Commando version of the M-16 assault rifle.

C & C: Command and control.

CG: Commanding general.

CIB: Combat infantry badge.

CID: Criminal investigation division.

CO: Commanding officer.

COSVN: Central Office for South Vietnam. This was the Viet Cong headquarters for all South Vietnam.

CS: Riot-control gas.

Cs or C Rats: Canned individual rations.

Cammies: Camouflaged jungle fatigues—blouses, pants, hard hats, or berets.

Cammo-stick: Dual-colored camouflage greasepaint in a metal tube.

Canister round: M-79 round containing numerous double-O buckshot.

Cav: Short for Cavalry.

Cherry: New, inexperienced soldier recently arrived in a combat zone.

Chi-Com: Designation for Chinese Communist or an item of Chinese Communist manufacture or origin.

Chieu Hoi: An enemy soldier who has rallied to the South Vietnamese government.

Chopper: Informal term for any helicopter.

Chopper pad: Designated landing or takeoff platform for one or more helicopters.

Chuck: Informal term describing the enemy, also Charlie, Mr. Charles, Victor Charles, or VC.

Clacker: Informal term describing the electric firing device for a claymore mine or a fougasse barrel.

Claymore mine: Command-detonated, antipersonnel mine designed to saturate an area six to eight feet above the ground and over an area of sixty degrees across its front, with 750 steel ball bearings.

Cockadau: Vietnamese slang derivative meaning "kill."

Cold: Term describing an area of operations or a landing zone that is devoid of any enemy sign or activity.

Commo: Communication.

Commo check: Radio operator's request to verify the reception of his transmissions.

Compromise: Enemy discovery of the presence of a LRP/Ranger in its vicinity, thereby resulting in the termination of the mission and the extraction of the team.

Concertina: Coiled barbed wire strung for perimeter defense.

Conex: Large steel container used to transport and store U.S. military supplies and equipment.

Contact: Firing on or being fired on by the enemy.

Contour flying: Low-level, high-speed, daring helicopter flight adjusting altitude only for terrain features.

Daisy chain: More than one claymore mine wired together with det cord to effect simultaneous detonation.

DEROS: Date of estimated return from overseas.

Det cord: Detonator cord, demolition cord: timed-burn fuse used with plastique explosives or to daisy-chain claymores together.

Deuce and a half: Two-and-one-half-ton military transport truck.

Dex tabs: Dexedrine tablets: an aid to prevent sleep; could cause hallucinations or wild, uncontrolled behavior if taken to excess.

Diddly bopping or diddy boppin': Slang term meaning "to move about foolishly and without taking security measures."

Di di or di di mau: Vietnamese phrase meaning "get out" or "go."

Dopers: Slang term for soldiers who use drugs; opposite of "juicers."

Double-canopy: Phrase used to describe primary jungle with a lower layer of undergrowth.

Dustoff: Helicopter conducting a medical evacuation.

E & E: Escape and evasion.

Early out: Termination of military service prior to normal ETS.

EM: Enlisted man.

ETS: Estimated termination of service.

Exfiltration: The procedure of departing a recon zone after completion of a mission.

Extraction: The removal of troops from the field, usually by helicopter.

F-4 (Phantom): McDonnell-Douglas fighter-bombers that saw heavy use in Vietnam.

FAC: Forward air controller.

FO: Forward observer.

FOB: Forward operation base.

Fast mover: U.S. fighter-bomber.

Firebase or **fire support base:** Forward artillery base.

Firefight: Small-arms battle.

Firefly: LOH scout helicopter, mounting a searchlight and capable of dropping aerial flares.

Fire mission: Directed artillery barrage.

Flak jackets: Vests worn by U.S. soldiers to lessen the severity of torso wounds caused by shrapnel.

Fougasse or **phoo gas:** A mixture of JP-4 aviation fuel and naphtha, which performed like napalm when detonated. It was placed in fifty-five-gallon drums and buried outside military perimeters as part of the front-line defense. Very effective against massed troops.

Frag: Fragmentation grenade.

Freedom bird: Name given to any military or commercial aircraft that took troops out of Vietnam.

Free-fire zone: An area declared off-limits to all personnel. Anyone encountered within its confines was assumed to be hostile and could be fired on without verification or authorization.

G-2: Division intelligence.

G-3: Division operations section.

Goofy grape: Slang for purple.

Gook: Derogatory slang term for any Oriental person, especially Viet Cong or NVA. Also dink, slope, slant, or zipperhead.

Go to cover: Move into heavy concealment.

Graves Registration: Section of the military service charged with reception, identification, and disposition of U.S. military dead.

Grunt: U.S. infantryman.

Gunship: Heavily armed helicopter used to support infantry troops or to independently attack enemy units or positions.

H & I: Harassment and interdiction, preplotted artillery fire designed to keep the enemy on edge and possibly catch him off balance.

HE: High explosive.

HQ: Headquarters.

Halazone tabs: Halazone tablets, used to purify water before consumption.

Heads: Slang term for soldiers who smoke marijuana.

Heat tabs: Heating tablets, small blue chemical discs that burned slowly and gave off an intense, smokeless heat when ignited. Used for heating rations and boiling water.

Heavy team: A LRP or Ranger team of ten or more personnel.

Helipad: (See acid pad or chopper pad.)

Ho Chi Minh trail: A vast network of roads and trails, running from southern North Vietnam, down through Laos, Cambodia, and South Vietnam and terminating just to the northwest of Saigon. It made up the transportation system that enabled the North Vietnamese Army to replace its losses of manpower, arms, and equipment.

Ho Chi Minhs: A slang name for the sandals worn by the Vietnamese, made from discarded automobile tires and inner tubes.

Hootch: Slang term for any small civilian family or military shelters in Vietnam.

Horn: Term used to describe radio communications.

Hot: Term describing an area of operations or a landing zone where contact has been made with enemy troops.

Huey: UH-1 helicopter, the primary helicopter troop transport in Vietnam.

Hump (the): The midpoint in a soldier's overseas combat tour, usually the 183d day.

Hump (to): To walk on patrol, usually heavily laden and heavily armed: to perform any difficult task.

I Corps: Northernmost military district in South Vietnam.

II Corps: Central military district in South Vietnam.

III Corps: Area around Saigon and north to Phuoc Long Province.

IV Corps: Southernmost military district in South Vietnam.

IG: Inspector General.

In-country: Term used to refer to American troops serving in Vietnam.

Indian country: The jungle, also known as the bush, boonies, boondocks, the field.

Infiltration: The procedure of entering a recon zone without detection by the enemy.

Insertion: The placement of combat or recon forces in the field, usually by helicopter.

Instant NCO or Shake 'N' Bake: Derogatory informal terms used to describe soldiers who received their rank as noncommissioned officers, not by time in service and time in grade, but by graduation from the NCO school in Fort Benning, Georgia.

Jody: Universal name for the guy back home who tries to steal the GI's girl while he is overseas.

Jungle penetrator: A metal cylinder with fold-out legs, attached by steel cable to a helicopter-mounted hoist, used to medically evacuate wounded soldiers from thick, jungle terrain.

K-bar: Type of military combat knife used primarily by the Marines, LRPs, and Rangers.

KIA: Killed in action.

Killer team: A LRP or Ranger team with the primary mission of inflicting casualties upon the enemy through the use of ambush or raid.

Kill zone: The target area of an ambush.

Kit Carson scout: Former VC/NVA soldier, repatriated to serve as a scout for U.S. combat forces.

Klick: One thousand meters, a kilometer.

LAW: Light antitank weapon: a single-shot, disposable rocket launcher. Marines referred to the LAW as a LAAW, for light antiarmor weapon.

LBE: Load-bearing equipment.

LOH or **LOACH:** Light observation helicopter.

LP: Listening post.

LRP: Long-range patrol.

LRRP: Long-range reconnaissance patrol: also a dehydrated ration used by special operations units.

LZ: Landing zone.

Landline or **LIMA-LIMA:** Ground telephone communications between two points.

Lay dog: Going to cover after insertion to wait and listen for any sign of enemy movement or presence in the area.

Lifer: A career soldier.

LIMA CHARLIE: The phonetic military designation for the letters *L* and *C* which are used as a reply to the radio commo request, "How do you read me?" It means "loud and clear!"

Lister bag: A waterproof canvas bag, suspended from a beam or a tripod, providing potable drinking water to troops in bivouac.

Lock 'n' load: To chamber a round in one's weapon.

Lurpin': Slang used to identify activity of LRP—LRRP—Rangers.

M-16: Lightweight automatic assault rifle used by U.S. forces in Vietnam: 5.56mm.

M-60: Light, 7.62mm, belt-fed machine gun used by U.S. forces in Vietnam.

M-79: Single-shot, 40mm grenade launcher: also called a blooper or a thumper.

MACV: Military Assistance Command, Vietnam.

MIA: Missing in action.

MP: Military police.

MPC: Military payment certificate(s): scrip, which GIs called funny money, issued to U.S. military personnel in Vietnam in place of

American bills and coins. This was done to hinder black-market activities since the military authorities could (and frequently did) call in all old MPC and exchange it for new bills of different appearance. The exchange would make worthless all the old scrip held by black marketeers if they were not warned in time of the impending currency exchange.

Mag: Ammunition magazine.

McGuire rig: A nylon sling or seat attached to a 120-foot rope, used to extract special operations personnel from dense jungle under extreme conditions.

Meal-on-wheels: Mobile snack trucks found at major U.S. military bases.

Medevac: Helicopter conducting a medical evacuation.

Mike: Phonetic military designation for the letter *M:* usually means minutes or meters.

Monsoon: The rainy season in the Orient.

NCO: Noncommissioned officer: ranks E-4 (corporal, but not Specialist 4) thru E-9 (sergeant major).

NCOIC: Noncommissioned officer in charge.

NDP: Night defense position.

NVA: North Vietnamese Army.

Nam or **the Nam:** Short for Vietnam.

Number one: Slang, means the very best.

Number ten: Slang, means the very worst.

Nuoc mam: Rotten-smelling fish sauce used by the Vietnamese.

OCS: Officer Candidate School.

OP: Observation post.

One-oh-five: 105mm howitzer.

One-five-five: 155mm artillery.

One-seven-five: 175mm artillery.

Op order: Operations order, a notice of an impending operation.

Overflight: Premission aerial scout of a recon zone for the purpose of selecting primary and secondary landing zones and extraction points, determining route of march, and locating possible trails and enemy supply depots, structures, and emplacements; usually conducted by the team leader and his assistant team leader. The inserting helicopter crew flies the overflight.

PAVN: People's Army of Vietnam, aka NVA. The standing army of North Vietnam.

PBR: "Patrol boat river"—small, highly maneuverable boat, with .50-caliber, .30-caliber, and M-60 machine guns, used to insert LRP–Ranger, Special Forces, and SEAL teams mainly in the Mekong Delta.

PF: Popular Forces: South Vietnamese irregular forces.

PFC: Private first class.

PLF: Parachute landing fall.

POW: Prisoner of war.

PRC-25 or **PRICK-25:** Portable radio used by American combat troops in the field.

PSP: Perforated steel plating used for airstrips, helicopter pads, bunker construction, and bridge matting.

PT: Physical training.

PX: Post exchange.

PZ: Pickup zone.

Peter Pilot: Copilot of a helicopter.

Piastres or **Ps:** Vietnamese currency.

Pig: Affectionate slang nickname for the M-60 machine gun.

Pink team: Airborne hunter-killer team consisting of one or more LOH scout helicopters, a Huey C & C helicopter, and two or more Cobra gunships.

Point: A unit's advance man in line of march, or the scout in a combat patrol.

Psy Ops: Psychological operations unit.

Pull pitch: Term used by helicopter pilots that means they are taking off.

Punji stakes: Sharpened bamboo stakes, hidden in grass, vegetation, in covered pits, or underwater, to penetrate the feet and lower legs of unwary troops. They were often dipped in feces to cause infection to the wound.

R & R: Rest and Recreation: five- to six-day out-of-country furloughs given to U.S. military personnel serving in a combat zone.

RPD: Communist-made, drum-fed, light machine gun used by the VC/NVA forces in Vietnam.

RPG: Communist-made handheld grenade launcher, firing a B-40 rocket; used by both the VC and the NVA, it was effective against U.S. armor, fixed emplacements, helicopters, patrol boats, and infantry.

RTO: Radiotelephone operator.

RZ: Recon or reconnaissance zone.

Radio relay or **Xray:** A communications unit, usually set up on a firebase, with the mission of relaying transmissions from units in the field to their rear commands.

Rappel: The controlled descent, by means of a rope, from a tall structure or a hovering helicopter.

Reaction force: A military unit established to respond quickly and determinedly to another unit's request for rescue or reinforcement; also called "Blues."

Rear seat: The gunner in a Cobra gunship, and in certain dual-seat fighter-bombers.

Recondo School: An exclusive training program, conducted by 5th Special Forces personnel in Nha Trang, which taught small unit special operations techniques to members of U.S., South Vietnamese, Korea, Thai, and Australian special operations units.

Redlegs: Informal name given to artillerymen.

Revetment: Sandbagged or earthen blast wall erected to protect aircraft and helicopters from shrapnel and blast caused by hostile mortars, artillery, rockets, thrown satchel charges, or demolitions.

Rock 'n' roll: A slang term used to describe the firing of a weapon on full automatic, as opposed to semiautomatic.

Ruck or **Rucksack:** Infantryman's backpack.

SAR: Search and rescue.

SFC: Sergeant first class: E-7.

SKS: Communist-made 7.62mm semiautomatic assault rifle used by the VC and the NVA in Vietnam.

SOG: (MACV) Studies and Observation Group; specialized in deep-penetration patrols across the borders into South Vietnam's neighboring countries.

SOI: Signal operating instructions; the booklet that contained the call signs and radio frequencies of all units in Vietnam.

SOP: Standard operating procedure.

Sapper: Specially trained enemy soldier, with the mission to penetrate the perimeters of U.S. and allied military installations by stealth, and then to cause as much damage as possible to aircraft, vehicles, supply depots, communication centers, command centers, and hard defense positions. He would utilize satchel charges, grenades, demolition charges, and RPGs to accomplish his mission; sapper attacks often preceded mass infantry assaults and took place under heavy shelling by their own mortar and rocket crews.

Selector switch: A three-position device on the M-16 and CAR-15 assault rifles, enabling the operator to choose safe, semiautomatic, or automatic fire merely by thumbing it in ninety-degree increments.

Short or **short-timer:** A term to describe a soldier whose time remaining in country is less than sixty days.

Single-canopy: Phrase used to describe low, dense jungle or forest growth, with no overhead cover from mature trees.

Sitrep: Situation report; regularly scheduled communication check between a unit in the field and its rear command element, to inform it of their present status.

Six: Radio call sign for a unit's commander.

Slack: The second position in a line of march or in patrol formation; also means "go easy on."

Slack jump: A rappel involving a short free fall before the commencing of a standard rappel.

Slick: Informal name for a Huey troop transport helicopter.

Smoke: Informal name for a smoke grenade; they came in a variety of colors, and were used to signal others, to mark positions, to determine wind direction, and to provide concealment.

Snake: Informal name for the Cobra gunship.

Snatch: To capture a prisoner.

Spider hole: A one-man, camouflaged enemy fighting position, often connected to other positions by means of a tunnel.

Spotter round: Artillery or mortar shell producing a dense cloud of white smoke; they were used to mark targets or to assist units in establishing their correct locations.

Stand-down: An infantry unit's return from the field to a firebase or base camp for rest and resupply.

Starlight scope: A night-vision device utilizing any ambient light source, such as stars, the moon, electric lights, distant flares, etc. to artificially illuminate the area within its range of view.

Stars and Stripes: U.S. military newspaper.

Strack: A term used to describe or designate the ideal in military dress, demeanor, and bearing.

TAOR: Tactical area of responsibility.

TDY: Temporary duty.

TL: Team leader.

TOC: Tactical operations center.

Tac air: Fighter-bomber capability of the air force, navy, and Marine air wings; as opposed to the strategic bombing capacity of the air force's B-52s.

Tanglefoot: Fields of barbed wire stretched tightly over a grid of metal stakes, approximately twelve inches above the ground; it was part of a perimeter's static defense and was designed to discourage rapid and uninterrupted penetration.

Tarmac: A term describing the hard-surface coating used to construct permanent airstrips, helicopter pads, and roads; the word comes from "tar" and "macadam."

Ten-forty-nine or **1049:** The U.S. military form for requesting a transfer to another unit.

Toe popper: A small, plastic, U.S.-made antipersonnel mine, designed to cripple rather than kill.

Tracer: Ammunition containing a chemical composition to mark the flight of projectiles by a trail of smoke or fire.

Triple-canopy: Phrase used to describe mature jungle or forest, with a third layer of ancient trees, often reaching heights of two hundred feet or more, and blocking out the sun.

Turncoat: One who has changed sides or betrays his allegiance.

Typhoon: An Asian hurricane.

Uncle Ho: Familiar title for Ho Chi Minh, the leader of North Vietnam.

VC, Viet Cong, or **Victor Charles:** Slang names describing members of the People's Army of Vietnam.

WIA: Wounded in action.

WP, willie peter, willie pete, or **willie papa:** White phosphorus grenades, mortar rounds, or artillery rounds that exploded into a spray of chemical fire, which ignited on contact with air, and could be doused only by removal of the source of oxygen.

Wait-a-minute vines: Strong, barbed ground creepers that caught at the boots and clothing of American soldiers, and retarded their forward movement.

Warning order: A directive that gives final approval for an upcoming mission.

White Mice: A derogatory slang term for the military police of the South Vietnamese government.

WORLD (the): The States, USA, home.

XO: Executive officer.

Xray team: (See radio-relay team.)

Zapped: Killed, slain in combat.

Index

Airborne training, 3–4
AK-47s, 14, 23, 73, 90, 99, 118, 162
Allen, Marty, 177
All-night perimeter guard, 17–19
Ames, Nancy, 177
Anderson, Roger, 56, 59, 63–64
Angel's Wing, 41, 116
Animals, 34–35, 38, 127, 141–143
An Loc, 158
An My, 56–59, 62
Ants, 27, 142–143
Arenas, Reynaldo, 130, 131, 209
Arlington, Texas, 3
Army, Department of the, 144
ARVN (Army of Republic of Vietnam), 57
A Shau Valley, 175
Assistant team leader (ATL), 11
Atomi, Japan, 148, 149
"Australian peel," 46
Australians, 122

B-52 Arc Light, 109, 159
BDA (battle damage assessment), 75
Bell Helicopter, 177
Bennett, Greg, 20, 23, 67–69
Bien Hoa, 6
Blankenship, Freddie, 150–151

Blume, James, 209
Boots, Jim A., 209
Bourland, Larry, 81
Bowie, Jim, 77
Boyle, James P., 209
Brooke Army Medical Center, 171–179
Busby, Robert, 139, 179–181

C-47 gunships, 126
Caig, Lyn, 193
Calhoun, Bernice, 211
Calhoun, David, 211
Cambodia, 32, 41, 48, 92, 95, 106, 116, 121, 158, 159, 183
Camp Zama, 170
Cannon, Michael, 154
CAR-15s, 138, 166
Carson, Edward, 209
Caveman basketball, 33
Cervantes, Raymond, 154
CIC school, 9, 53, 54
Claymore mines, 27, 51, 59, 88, 89, 102
Climate, 17, 37, 84
Closson, Lawrence D., 128
Cobra gunships, 14, 23, 35, 85, 108, 154, 167, 181
Cohn, William P., Jr., 56, 209
Coleman, Al, 56

227

Company F, 52d Infantry (LRP),
    1st Infantry Division, xviii,
    xxi, 7, 9, 55, 57, 144, 196,
    209
Company F, 58th Infantry (LRP),
    101st Airborne Division,
    128
Company H, 75th Infantry
    (Ranger), 144
Company I, 75th Infantry (Ranger),
    xviii, xxi, 144, 196, 209
Company L, 75th Infantry
    (Ranger), 144
Contact front, 46
Conyers, Private First Class,
    94–95, 98
Cook, Carl, xvii–xix, 92, 93, 129,
    130, 168
COSVN (Central Office for South
    Vietnam), 159, 160
Coyle, Gerard, 209
Crabtree, Barry, 179–185
Crawley, 139
Crews, Ron, 20, 22, 130, 131, 156
Crockett, Davy, 77
Crow, Philip, 175–176
Cruz, Enrique S., 157, 158, 160,
    162, 163, 165, 210

Davis, Jerry, 53–54, 129, 130, 136,
    137, 145, 157, 168
DC-3 gunships, 65
Defensive perimeter, 49
Defoliation, 81–83
Di An, 20, 123, 150, 151
Dinoto, Merle, 211
Dinoto, Mike, 211
Doan, Lester A., 209
Dog Leg Village, 56–59, 62, 64
Dong Ap Bia (Hamburger Hill),
    175
Douglas, John, 130, 131
Dustoff helicopter, 103, 130

"Echoes of Freedom" (Goshen),
    201–203

XVIII Airborne Corps, 5
82d Airborne Division, 4–5, 128
Elsner, Robert, 56, 59, 60, 63, 64,
    194, 195

F-4 Phantoms, 90, 110
FAC (forward air controller)
    spotter plane, 61, 62
Ferris, Chris, 56, 64
5th Mech Division, 128
5th NVA Division, 159
5th Special Forces Group, 6, 122,
    128
Firefly, 61
Fire Support Base Coral, 65
1st Cavalry Division, 128, 144
1st Infantry Division (Big Red
    One), xviii, 7, 8, 10, 29, 32,
    55, 56, 65, 67, 71, 76, 93,
    98, 110, 115, 128, 129,
    144, 150, 157, 169, 179,
    192–197, 209–210
    G-2 (Intelligence), 56, 57, 64,
    69, 70
    1st Battalion, 26th Infantry, 64
    1st Battalion, 28th Infantry, 56
    1st Squadron, 4th Cavalry, 56,
    61
1st Royal Australian Regiment, 65
Fishhook, the, 158, 159
Force Recon Diary, 1970 (Norton),
    35*n*
Ford, Judith Ann, 176
Fort Benning, Georgia, 3, 196
Fort Bragg, North Carolina, 4, 123
Fort Huachuca, Arizona, 3
Fort Polk, Louisiana, 3, 153
Fort Sam Houston, Texas, 171, 188
4th Infantry Division, 128
Freedom Bird, 38
Friendly fire, 108

Gatling guns, 75
Gerber, Steve, 2–3
Ghosting, 17
Gnats, 143

Goshen, Jackie Coble, 187–189, 211
Goshen, Kurt, 189
Goshen, Wendy, 189
Grand Summit Mountain, 126

Halazone tablets, 88–89
Hamburger Hill, 175
Hansen, Captain, 181
Harper, Timothy V., 210
Harris, Sergeant, 25, 99
Hartsoe, Charlie, 20–23, 56, 64, 67–70
Hayashi, Rodney, 20, 67, 68, 151
Henry, Mrs. (Mama Cass), 176–177
Highway 4, 159
Highway 7, 159
Highway 13 (Thunder Road), 21, 22, 48, 55, 150, 159
Hildebrandt, Don "Giant," 52, 71–73, 85–86, 150–151, 157
Hill, Dave, 56, 62
Hobo Woods, 101, 193
Hurst, Texas, 87, 177

I Corps, 175
I Field Force, 7
II Field Force, 7
III Corps, 7–8, 86, 92
Indians, 44–45
Irving, Texas, 2
Isaacs, Vaughn, 10, 20, 21, 134
IV Corps, 92

Japan, 145–149
Johnson, Gary L., 157, 163–165, 168, 169, 210

Kampong Cham Province (the Fishhook), 158, 159
Kernan, Mike R., 210
Khmer Rouge, 106
KIA symbol, 211–212
Kirby, George, 177

Kirby, Tony, 20, 22, 67, 68, 70
Knowlton, George F., 194, 209

Lai Khe, 8, 13, 20, 25, 28, 33, 38, 39, 43, 48, 76, 79, 82–84, 86, 91, 94, 98, 100, 103, 110, 112, 114–115, 120, 128, 129, 134, 150–153, 158, 159, 168, 193, 194
Laos, 32, 106, 121, 158, 175
"Last Team, The" (Goshen), 199–200
Law, Robert D. "Outlaw," 152–157, 209
Leeches, 142, 161
Levine, Robert P., 157–158, 165, 210
Liebnitz, James T., 157, 165, 210
Liesure, Jack G., 56, 58–60, 62–64, 66, 209
Loc Ninh, 21
Long Binh, 6
Long Nguyen Secret Zone, 92
Lowry, Bob, 150–152, 157
Luse, Ronnie, 56–60, 62–64

M-14E2s, 59
M-16s, 12, 59, 100, 108, 138, 166
M-60s, 14, 114, 136–138, 179
M-70s, 12
MACV Recondo School, 52, 122–128
MACV-SOG, 159
Markovitch, Anthony G., 151, 210
MASH unit, 86, 103, 150, 152, 181
Massey, Sergeant, 157
Mattoon, Steve "Cahuna," 92–94, 98–100, 107, 109, 129, 130
Medal of Honor, 155–156
Michelin rubber plantation, 25, 179
Mills, John, 56, 62
Moll, Joseph, 172, 178
Moncrief, Brigadier General, 176
Montagnards, 159, 193, 194

Morse code school, 3
Mosquitoes, 141–142, 161
Mount Fuji, 147, 148
Mulholland, Arnold L., 209

Newcombe, 185
Nha Trang, 122, 123, 127
9th Infantry Division, 128
90th Replacement Center, 6
North Texas State University, 2
North Vietnamese Army (NVA), 9,
    38, 45, 55–58, 60, 62–65,
    70, 92, 98, 100, 105, 106,
    112, 121, 126, 129, 151,
    157–160, 162–168, 175,
    180, 184–184
Norton, Doc, 35n
Nunez, Rudolph A., 209

101st Airborne Division, 128, 144,
    175, 196
173d Airborne Brigade, 128
199th Light Infantry Brigade, 128
Outhouses, 17
Owens, Buck, 177

Pathet Lao, 106
Patrick, Reese M., 210
PBRs ("patrol boat, river"), 139,
    140
Peck, Ken, 211
Peck, Ramona, 211
Phantom factor, 28–30
Phnom Penh, 159
Phu Loi, 55–59, 61, 62, 64, 65,
    67–69
Physical training, 10, 79, 103,
    123–124
Point man, 36–37, 46
Powell, Bill, 154, 155
POWs, 45
PRC-25 radios, 13, 28, 68, 69,
    167
Project Delta, 122
Propson, Bernard A., 210
Puff the Magic Dragon, 75, 126

Quan Loi, 20, 159, 183–186

Rach Thi Thanh, 93
Randall, Michael, 210
Ranger creed, 96–97
Ranger school, 136
Ray, Lonnie, 8–9, 13, 26, 27, 41,
    42, 99, 100
Recondo School, 52
Rescue missions, 45–46
Rincon, Julian, 139
Rodrigues, Roberto, 123
Roossien, Robert A., 154, 155,
    183, 185–186, 210
RPGs (rocket-propelled grenades),
    18, 94, 137

Saigon, 55, 56, 58, 65, 146
Saigon River, 107–109
San Antonio, 77
Sandbagging, 17
Sappers, 18
Screaming Eagles, 175
SEALs, 12, 128
Second Tet Offensive, 157
7th NVA Division, 159
75th Infantry (Ranger), 144, 196
Sidewinder, 90
Sihanoukville, 159
Silva, Fred, 8, 25, 53–54
Smith, Charles E., Jr., 210
Smith, Don, xiii–xv
Smoke Bomb Hill, 5
Snakes, 34–35, 85, 86, 141, 143
Song Be, 87, 154, 155
Song Be Corridor, 151, 158
Sorick, Steven, 194, 209
South Koreans, 122, 125–126
Special Forces (SF), 3–5, 7, 12,
    52, 101, 122, 126, 153,
    154
Spooky, 65
Stars & Stripes, 134
Suive, Harry (Frenchie), 81, 123,
    128, 179
Sullivan, Ed, 177

Suoi Ong Bang tributary, 155
Sweeney, Phil, 67, 68

Tanks, 76, 110
Tan Son Nhut Airport, 6, 149
Tapia, John, 193
Team 11, 94–95, 98
Team 5, 93, 94
Team 4, 94
Team leader (TL), 11
Team 9, 93
Team 10, 93
Team 3, 93
Team Victim Eight, 160–169
Team Wildcat 1, 52, 55–58, 61–65, 157
Team Wildcat 7, 20–24, 67–70
Team Wildcat 2, 55–65
Tet Offensive, 56, 58
Thais, 122
Thunder Base Two, 81, 151
Thunder Road, 21, 22, 48, 55, 150, 159
TOT (time on target) barrage, 61, 62
Trang, 52
Trapezoid, the, 92, 107
Travis, William, 77
Travis Air Force Base, 170

Tu Duc water plant, 139
Tulsa, Oklahoma, 1
25th Infantry Division, 128, 179, 180
275th Infiltration Group, 65

United States wars, statistics of, 207

Viet Cong (VC), 9, 13–14, 21, 22, 25, 38, 40, 42, 45, 49, 55–57, 70, 72–76, 81, 84, 90–95, 98–100, 103–106, 109–112, 114, 117–121, 131, 137, 138, 140, 154, 155, 159, 160, 180

"Wall Talk" (Goshen), v–vii
War Zone C, 158
War Zone D, 158
Washington, Anthony F., 94, 209
Washington, George, 191
Welch, Colonel, 4
Wenzel, Larry, 157, 163, 165–171, 176, 190
Westmoreland, General, 122, 132
Whiting, Kenneth, 123, 128
Wiggins, Daniel, 139, 154
Womack Army Hospital, 5

Look for Gary Linderer's two books on LRRPs, LRPs and Rangers in gut-chilling, extreme combat far behind enemy lines. When every mission may well have been their last, these brave men went willingly into harm's way with only their skill, sense of duty, personal weapons, and each other between themselves and death.

Phantom Warriors Book I and Book II: LRRPs, LRPs, and Rangers in Vietnam

by Gary A. Linderer

Published by Ballantine Books.
Available at a bookstore near you.